ISBN 978-0-9582863-5-0

90000

9 780958 286350

I0042250

AB Publishing House, Auckland Sydney Chennai,

Email: abpublish@gmail.com

Printed in the United States of America

First Printing: 2010

ABOUT THIS BOOK

Astrological Real Life Q & Answers- For Applied Astrology and Practice

Vedic Astrology Analysed with charts from user questions   By Mr. Natarajan S

Ranked 1st in 24 categories - Ranked 21st in over 10,000 Featured Astrologers in Ammas, Ranked by Top Astrologers and users as on 14-01-2010 and Council member in 7 categories

As given by S. Natarajan (R.S.) in various online forums including Ammas (He was ranked 21 among 18000 Astrologers registered). He got over 35 years experience in Astrology. Way back in 1984 he with Wing Commander R.Ramakrishnan, developed Astrological charting software, rarity at that time.

He wrote several Sani Peyarchi, Guru Peyarchi books.He is Practicing Astrology for over 30 years.

He got training from Dr. C.S. Seshadri, direct disciple of Krishna Murthi Paththathi,. Puliyur Balu and Dr. B.V. Raman were his inspirations.

Some of his Spirutual gurus are his own maternal Grandma Avudai alias Gomathi, who was a sooth sayer with good following, Sri Sathya Sai Baba, Ramana Maharishi, Osho, Sankaracharya, J.K., Sri Aurobindo and Yogi Ram Surat Kumar.

Now he is in Australia. He gives astrological solutions through phone, email, and websites to corporate clients apart from his other activities.

Real names and places are suppressed for privacy in the questions.

This book will be of use for everybody especially for

- General reading- readers will acquire substantial knowledge in Astrology, from the bird's eye-view rather than from the basics, in interpreting charts in the professional way.

- Reference guide in Applied Vedic Astrology for Astrology Students and Researchers

- Cross reference guide as worked out examples for Professionals

- Cross reference as worked out examples for Astrology teachers

The author got top rankings in other 42 category subjects other than Astrology also please see the list at the backside

FROM THE AUTHOR:

Pranams at the feet of all of you as the Vedic Philosophy says "Each and Every one on this universe is God". Differences are for the sake of enjoyment.This book is from the answers I have given to people in online forums like Ammas where people seek relief form their problems, some want to know their future.

Ammas is a great forum; please feel free to support it.Thanks for all people who post their questions there and other great consultants who work very hard to solve problems of the Society. To follow strict privacy policy no names are given for the questions. Any other name given is to be taken as non representing any living or dead beings.

This compilation is chiefly for educational purposes for young and energetic Astrologers to understand Astro predictions from bird's eye-view from real life questions and answers. I have included many charts also for easy understanding. I have analysed as much as possible by the time and urgency.

I thought this could be useful for Astro minded

People as worked out reference.For general public, most frequenting problems are analysed from the angle of one horoscope.But mostly they can undertand the principles involved in problem solving.

My salutes are at the feet of Bhagawan Sathya Sai Baba. My pranams are to my mother T.S. Krishnambal, my father-in-law Er.K.Sundaram and Prof A.V.Dharmapadam.

Sincere thanks goes -for supporting me in many ways: to my beautiful wife Latha Maheswari, son Abishek, & daughter Sai Kiran AND to my service minded brothers and sisters Sankar, Ramakrishnan, Latha and Gomathi & to their children AND to my energetic sister-in-law Mrs. Parvathavardhani and Mr.Narayanan.

S.Natarajan

PRAYER LIST FOR THE WELFARE OF SERVICE MINDED PEOPLE AMONGST US.

My dear readers please join me in prayers for the welfare of the first batch of some great people doing unostentatious service. May God bless the friends and relatives below!! May God bless all of you, my readers with happiness!

MR&Mrs.R. Krishnan,Madipakkam, Mr&Mrs.S.G.Ethirajan,Tiruporur Mr&Mrs.S.G. Parthasarathy, Mr&Mrs.V.P.Kathiravan of V.P.S. Printers, Prof.&Mrs.R. Murali,Madurai Mr.&Mrs.Jayaraman,Srinivasanagar, Mr&Mrs.Deivasigamani,Kancheepuram, Mrs&Mrs.Sundaram,Chromepet, Mr&Mrs. A.Venkatraman,Sydney, Mr&Mrs.Joseph Willson,Sydney, Mr&Mrs.C.S.Venkateswaran,Madipakkam, Mrs.Rajeswari, Mrs.Lydia John Chakravarthy, Dr&Mrs. Venkatesh Mahadevan,Australia, Mr&Mrs.T.Parthasarathy, Er& Dr.Suresh,UK, Er&Mrs.Chander,U.K., Mr&Mrs.Aziz, Mr&Mrs.J.Gopalakrishnan,Mylapore, Mr&Mrs.Ayyappan, Mr.H.S.Mani, Mr&Mrs.M.Sankar, Mr&Mrs.S.Sankar, Mrs&Mrs.Somu,Chromepet, Mrs.Gomathi&Mr.Narayanan, Mrs.Meena&Mr.Ravi Shankar,Bangalore, Mr&Mrs.K.Anandan, Mr.T.S.Kanthamani Mama and Muthu Mami,Miss Mangala, Mrs.Mohana&Mr.Srinivasan, Lalitha Chiththi, Mr&Mrs.Ganesan,Virugambakkam, Wg.Cdr.Shyam&Mrs.Rama, Auckland, Drs.Subramanians,Auckland, Meho and Enisa, Mr&Mrs.J.Srinivasan,Auckland, Mr&Mrs.Sridhar Dharmapadam,Kuwait,Mr&Mrs.Sankara,Annanagar, Mr&Mrs.Srinath, USA, Mr&Mrs.Sriram, Hongkong, Miss P.S.Sasikala and family,Mylapore

Mrs.Latha, Financial Advisor, Auckland, Mr&Mrs.David Rodriguez, Mr&Mrs.David Karthik,Mr&Mrs.Nithin Seth, Mr.&Mrs.Anil Varandhani, Sydney, Aussie Singer Tom and Family, Lionell family from Paris,The hard working brothers and sisters in Rakon, Cochlear, One Tree Hill College,Te Papapa School, Arthur Phillips School, LSGHSS, MES School-Qatar, Windows2000 -Muscat, Service minded Sai Seva Samithi workers-Howick,Strathfield,Wentworthville and all over the world, Everybody associated with Sydney Ayyappa Temple, Sydney Muruga Temple, Hare Krishna Temple, Hellensville

If you want your friend/relative who does such service to be

included in the list in the next books please email me their particulars and service they do to:
unostentatiouslist@yahoo.com.au

CONTENTS

Other generes authored by him

SO POWERFUL - IMMORTAL LOVE POEMS FOR ALL AGES SO POWERFUL - IMMORTAL LOVE POEMS FOR ALL AGES (BOOK)

This is a collection of Free form Love Poems by a single author touching many aspects of love and ages with good lay out to cheer and relax you for a while from the stresses of day to day life. A good travel companion S.Natarajan's poems got over 6 million hits on internet

SO POWERFUL "THE INDIAN LOVE"SO POWERFUL "THE INDIAN LOVE" (BOOK)

This book gives you vivid picture of what happened in India between Raj and Latha during 1982 – This book is to cheer you for a short reading. This is a modern style unique attempt by "A poet's diary notes" by S.Natarajan with millions of hit for his writing. This book has got literary value for it is depicting the yesteryear of India from Madras angle. Travel companion book

FREEDOM AND OUR MINDSFREEDOM AND OUR MINDS (BOOK)

THE PHILOSOPHY THAT TAKES YOU TO YOUR INNER CORE FROM THE BIG PICTURE WORLD CONSCIENCE

My Views on Issues in New Zealand & other countries 2007-2008 My Views on Issues in New Zealand & other countries 2007-2008 (book)

INTERESTING VIEWS ON INTERESTING CONTEMPORARY TOPICS OF NEW ZEALAND AND OTHER COUNTRIES

CDs

FREEDOM AND OUR MINDS CD-1 FREEDOM AND OUR MINDS CD-1 (CD)

Do you know whether your mind is your friend or enemy? Indian Philosophy which is thousands of years old shows the path to understand our true potential and achieve our determined paths in life. The talks given by enlightened S.Natarajan will give inside out of Vedanta, Indian philosophy and easy to follow Jyoti meditation. These will pave the way for your success in all spheres of life. This is first part containing these tracks: 1. True Freedom 2.The Three Stages 3. The Lion Stage 4.Kundalini and our Mind 5.Pure Love is meditation 6.Jyoti meditation Practice track 7.Curing Illness spiritually The second cd contains 1.You become what you think 2. Always try a little more 3.Why and how we become old 4.Breath and light in Meditation 5 to 8 Indian Philosophy in a Nutshell part 1-4, 9.Luck or fate 10.Mind chattering

FREEDOM
AND OUR
MINDS
CD-2

FREEDOM AND OUR MINDS CD-2FREEDOM AND OUR MINDS CD-2 (CD)

Do you know whether your mind is your friend or enemy? Indian Philosophy which is thousands of years old shows the path to understand our true potential and achieve our determined paths in life. The talks given by enlightened S.Natarajan will give inside out of Vedanta, Indian philosophy and easy to follow Jyoti meditation. These will pave the way for your success in all spheres of life. The first part contains these tracks: 1. True Freedom 2.The Three Stages 3. The Lion Stage 4.Kundalini and our Mind 5.Pure Love is meditation 6.Jyoti meditation Practice track 7.Curing Illness spiritually The second cd contains 1.You become what you think 2. Always try a little more 3.Why and how we become old 4.Breath and light in Meditation 5 to 8 Indian Philosophy in a Nutshell part 1-4, 9.Luck or fate 10.Mind chattering

FLOWERISHFLOWERISH ( )
FLOWERS IN NEW PLYMOUTH PARK

All these books/cds are available in paper form as well electronic form for online ordering.

Visit www.abpublishinghouse.com

Or for consulting on Public domain

http://cheersammas.com

ARTICLES:

1.CONCEPTION AND MISCONCEPTION OF KUJA DOSHA
24 Jul 09

Marriages are made in heaven.

In Vedic Astrology what should be considered?

There are several conceptions and misconceptions about Kuja Dosha.

Who is or what is Kuja?

Puranik talks about Karthikeya, the warrior, as the lord of Mars. These apart - Mars is considered a fire and war planet world over and its position in one's 1,2,4,7,12 houses is considered to affect that house.

What is Kuja Dosha?

A calculation shows that as many as 90% of the people in the world will be under the influence of Kuja Dosha. If so, is it real or is it just a hollow concept.

Kuja dosha in horoscope

One of the biggest misconceptions and fears in the Hindu society with respect to marriage is the presence of Kuja Dosha in the natal horoscope. Kuja dosha occurs, when Kuja is placed in the ascendant, 4th, 7th, 8th or 12th house of the natal chart. However, majority of the astrologers include the 2nd house also in the Kuja dosha list. People in whose natal chart Kuja is placed in the above positions are under the influence of Kuja.

Kuja is considered to be a commander-in-chief among all planets. It symbolizes immense courage, aggression, vitality, fire, confidence and warrior qualities. It drives the fire of independent spirit and sense of purpose among individuals.

Ascendant or raising sign is about the person, and second is about one's family and fourth house is Suha sthana, Seventh house is about partner and eighth house is about longevity of life as well as partner's life, twelfth house is about happiness in bed.

When Mars is situated in 1,2,4,7,8,12 the house of ascendant/ Moon sign, you would have now understood the firey qualities will affect those houses, which will affect the marriage relationship.

Now we will see what Kuja can do in these houses

- Kuja in the first house: quarrelsome on even minor issues; combative and dominating in relationship.

- Kuja in the 2nd house: harsh speech.

- Kuja in the 4th house: aggressive independent nature, which may affect the Suha between them

- Kuja in the 7th house: a lot of energy; differences with family members, difference of opinion with mate

- Kuja in the 8th house: early death of the mate.

- Kuja in the 12th house: financial losses, many enemies and repressed anger, aggressive nature in bed

According to Brihat Parasara Hora Shastra, if Kuja is placed in the lagna, 4th, 7th, 8th and 12th houses, without any aspect or conjunction of the benefit planets, then the husband of such women certainly have an early death. Hence it is understood that if Kuja has an aspect of a benefit or is conjunct with a benefit, then the dosha is mostly reduced.

An exception to this however exists. "If a woman with the widowhood yoga marries a man with a similar yoga of loss of spouse, then such yoga will get cancelled." Hence the second exception given by him is that Kuja Dosha is canceled, if both the girl and the boy have Kuja Dosha.

The way out of Kuja Dosha is for a person with Kuja Dosha to marry another with Kuja Dosha

"The most significant problem is that, a person with a Kuja Dosha will not feel much physical attraction to another with Kuja Dosha"

Exceptions to Kuja dosha

Kuja dosha gets canceled in some special conditions as defined below:

Some of them have good reasons some of them don't. We will come to analysing them later.

These are some general Exceptions

When Kuja is in its own sign Mesha, exalted Karkataka or in the houses owned by planets considered to be his friend's viz., Ravi, Guru and Chandra-

If Kuja is in the 2nd house, but in the signs of Mithuna or Kanya (I say in those signs Mars loses its fiery qualities).

If Kuja is in the 4th house, but in Mesha

If Kuja is in the 7th house, but in Karkataka or Makara

If Kuja is in the 8th house, but in Pisces

If Kuja is in the 12th house, but in Vrushaba or Tula

For Karkataka and Simha lagnas, Kuja is yoga Karaka and so no dosha wherever it is placed.

For Kumba lagna, if Mars is in the 4th or 8th house.

If benefic Guru or Sukra occupies the ascendant

If Kuja is in conjunction or aspected by Guru or Chandra

If Kuja is in conjunction or aspected by Ravi, Budha, Sani or Rahu

Kuja Dosha is considerably reduced, if Sani aspects the houses owned by Kuja, but subject to the other planetary positions in the natal chart. Remember that even if a person has severe Kuja Dosha, after the age of 28, the effects of Kuja Dosha are reduced

Mangalik Dosh effects seems to be more severe in the natal charts, where Mars becomes functional malefic i.e. Virgo, Scorpio and Taurus ascendant charts.

If both the bride and bridegroom have Kuja in 2,4,7,8,12 positioned, there is no Kuja dosha.

Age at which marriage occurs

There is a concept that after 28years Kuja Dosha need not be considered.

Arranged or Love Marriage

Apart from all these above, there is a belief that for Kandharva Marriage, not arranged by elders, if the love is for substantial no.of years - that is if the boy and girl love each other so much, there is no need to consider Kuja Dosha, as it is decided by God, nobody can interfere.

Tell me which side of the wall you are now....Manglik or non Manglik

2.SADE SATI. FIRST, SECOND, THIRD AND FOURTH
05 Aug 09

Saturn takes 30 years to orbit all the 12 houses. Three such cycles in one's life will be between 60 years to 90 years, based on where Saturn was at the time of birth in relation to Moon.

The first cycle of Sadhesati of Saturn is extremely intense and during this period you may experience physical pain. There would be obstacles and hardships of various kinds. During this period of Sadhesati, there may also be some troubles to your parents.

In the second cycle of Sadhesati, Saturn exerts mediocre influence compared to first cycle. During this period you succeed through physical struggle and labor. Despite mental unrest, your worldly progress continues. You may suffer separation or loss of parents or other elders in the family. In Tamil they call it "Pongu Sani" meaning it is progression for the native.

In the third cycle of Sadhesati, Saturn inflicts extremely harsh results. During this period you may face tremendous physical hardships. There will be illness and even fear of death. During this period only fortunate persons survive. In Tamil they call it "Mangu Sani" meaning it is regression for the native.

What about people living after 90 years? Normally Saturn will not do any harm to them. It will help them to attain the reasoning of life principles.

In general Saturn is Karaka for life. When he is creating problem, we call it life and death problem. But his intention is never to kill. It is to correct us and lead us into the right path. He supports every charitable effort of yours. If at all you want to satisfy Saturn, then turn to poor and needy, you will be given the best possible protection by even the most feared Saturn.

3. WHO HAS THE KNOWLEDGE OF COSMOS?
26 Jul 09

Carl Sagan was a notable Scientist- Sagan's capability to convey his ideas allowed many people to better understand the cosmos— simultaneously emphasizing the value and worthiness of the human race, and the relative insignificance of the earth in comparison to the universe. He delivered the 1977 series of Royal Institution Christmas Lectures at the Royal Institution in London. He hosted and, with Ann Druyan, co-wrote and co-produced the highly popular thirteen-part PBS television series Cosmos: A Personal Voyage modeled on Jacob Bronowski's The Ascent of Man.

Sagan with a model of the Viking Lander probes which would land on Mars. Sagan examined possible landing sites for Viking along with Mike Carr and Hal Masursky.

Cosmos covered a wide range of scientific subjects including the origin of life and a perspective of our place in the universe. The series was first broadcast by the Public Broadcasting Service in 1980, winning an Emmy and a Peabody Award. It has been broadcast in more than 60 countries and seen by over 600 million people, according to the Science Channel. [16]

A galaxy is composed of gas and dust and stars — billions upon billions of stars.

—Carl Sagan, Cosmos, chapter 1, page 3[20]

"Those worlds in space are as countless as all the grains of sand on all the beaches of the earth. Each of those worlds is as real as ours and every one of them is a succession of incidents, events, occurrences which influence its future. Countless worlds, numberless movements, an immensity of space and time; And our small planet at this moment, here we face a critical branch point in history, what we do with our world, right now, will propagate down through the centuries and powerfully affect the destiny of our descendants, it is well within our power to destroy our civilisation and perhaps our species as well. "

The US unmanned Mars Pathfinder spacecraft was renamed the Carl Sagan Memorial Station on July 5, 1997, which shows the significance of this great Scientist.

He wanted to start the "Cosmos" serial with a good beginning. For that he looked at cultures/civilisations for the best knowledge about Cosmos. He started researching the civilisations of Greek, Sumaria, Egypt, Rome, Babylon, but he was not satisfied. Then he looked into civilisations in relation to their

Religion and Epics. When he researched Hindu civilisation and Hindu epics and vedas, he was astonished about the knowledge of cosmos in them.

Indians were the first inventors of ZERO. They found ZERO added after any number can make numerical expressions easy.

He found that in the Cosmos, even big numbers become expressionless. When he talked about stars etc. he used to tell Billions and billions, with lot of criticism by others.

When he looked at the civilisations which were able to express the cosmos numerically well he found Hindu religion has plenty to offer.

Hindu literature talks like Sangam, Padmam for big nos. In Mahabharath these are the words to indicate big nos.

Ayutham = 10,000

Prayutham = 10,00,000

Sangu = 10000000000000

Padmam = 1000000000

Arputham = 100000000

Garvam = 10000000000

Sangam = 1000000000000

Nigarvam = 100000000000

Mahapadmam= 1000000000000000

Madyam = 10000000000000000

Prartham =100000000000000000

Such unthinkable numbers at that time were normally mentioned only in Hindu Religious literature and civilisations related to cosmos.

Again Carl Sagan wondered about the mention and the clear understanding of Yuga, Kalpam in our literature. He is astonished by our knowledge on the unending cycle of beginning and end of Cosmos (Pralaya)

He says " Only Hindu religion has thorough knowledge about the cyclical nature of beginning, and end at the Pralaya and rebirth of cosmos. This totally tallies with modern Cosmos research and understanding. It mentions about normal days, months and calculates and talks about -8.64 billion years. The knowledge goes beyond the age of Earth, Sun and Moon and very much beyond the Big Bang theories. It is the ultimate to mention about the ultimate of beyond and beyond.

He was wondering why Hindu Civilisation and religion are still lively when all other old civilisations are no more. His travel to India to find out the truth revealed more information about Cosmos in our Vedas.

He explained the mystery of Cosmos showing (Chidambaram) Natarajar.

He found his notions about Cosmos are already there in Hindu Vedas of limitless cosmos and unlimited creativity which expands and expands without boundaries.

During the Hindu belief of Pralaya the opposite happens - the shrinking no of Billions and Billions of Stars and planets are really countless.

The Astronomy that we have in modern times is found to be the tiniest knowledge possible in contrast to the generic knowledge of Cosmos by Hindu civilisation.

What about astrology??? Can it be a real science if the above understanding can be put into relational aspects? I will discuss later on when time permits.

4. COURAGE AND BRAVERY ARE THE ALMA MATER FOR ARIES -

14 Aug 09

(Aries Moon, Lagna or Sun sign)

Bravery thy name is Aries

If you see persons who are optimistic, independent, impulsive, playful, competitive, courageous, a bit combative and adventurous, you can identify them as born in ARIES, Sun Sign.

Unlike Indian Vedic Astrology, Western systems give more importance to Sun sign. Here we talk about Aries as Sun sign OR Ascendant or Moon sign.

Try...try new things and run Enterprises

Aries people (lagna, moon sign or Sun sing Aries) start new things or new projects. They are fine entrepreneurs because they command the workforce under them. They often have trouble with authority above them and do better as their own bosses. They are good at self-promotion,(World Wrestling E/F championships and boasting wrestlers there-you get a good picture of the Aries personality) which ensures that many succeed in their own businesses.

Risk Takers to the core

Aries born, they can leap before looking and will take risks that others will never take. A courage- by -physical sign, that many Aries people take up risky professions like military, police force, stunt work, sports, strong politicians, rescue work or race-car driving. Aries people are emotionally courageous to the point of recklessness and will change their entire lives on a whim in order to follow some dream or romantic inclination.

Fast and furious:

Have you heard about Martial Arts named after mars? Aries people are really fast because they work on impulse. They tend to be accident-prone, not because they are clumsy but because they move quickly and impulsively. Aries people like to drive fast and many have an interest in extreme or high-impact sports or Martial Arts. Aries people crave the adrenaline rush of novelty and will often take unnecessary risks in order to achieve it.

Motorised:

The sign of Aries is associated with fast movement and engines. Many people with the sun, moon or ascendant in Aries are good with anything that has a motor. Many Aries people are drawn to professions or pastimes behind the wheels or wings (cars, flight)

Why details? Give me the plan!

Aries people are not particularly suited to detail work. They can't listen and plan. Typical Martian rather prefers to implement any big plans or he/she can start things to have others fill in the details. Listen to them with that arrogant authority, when they come up with creative ideas on the spot but they have trouble sustaining the effort to follow through with their plans unless the ascendant or moon is in an Earth sign (Taurus, Virgo or Capricorn) or in the water sign of Cancer or Scorpio.

No to Boredom in Aries company:

Push Aries born to the least boredom threshold they can lose interest in things quite easily. Come on give them a career with lots of change, social interaction and excitement or the Aries will want to move on.

Energy extraordinary and Athletic Awakening:

Their every day is loaded with super energy, which they need to burn off continuously through physical activities and socializing. They are competitive by nature and challenging .Good candidates for athletics, either team sports or solitary fitness activities. Most also enjoy watching sports and other physical displays such as dance, skating, skiing or other fitness activities that require movement and coordination. Their mantra is martial arts.

Explicit and Friendly

Aries people are extroverts and also very sociable. They like to be around other people most of the time and seek out novel and exciting situations. They prefer people who challenge them intellectually and compete with them in some way, and they quickly grow bored and irritated with homebodies and cautious, timid types.

Now the C word - Combat

Aries people think fast, move fast and talk fast (it becomes a style mostly liked by their Mars negative friends). They are not tolerant to slow moving, slow speaking people. In fact, Aries is the least patient sign of the zodiac.

If you see some Politicians talking down the other speakers in any Parliament you got a clue of what it would look like.

Force to rejuvenate

Aries people are forceful and even aggressive when pursuing what they want, and willing to charge head first into conflict. They prefer to deal with problems immediately, head on, and will rarely avoid confrontation. This leads them to poke at and provoke some of the more avoidant types. Aries people often have little respect for those who can't put up a good fight.

Honesty that others think as Rudeness

Aries people tend to be honest and forthright, almost to a fault at times. They are not subtle, and they have terrible tempers that are easily set off, though they are also quick to forgive. They often say and do things rashly that cause strife in their interpersonal relationships. A lack of tact can create problems. When bored, Aries people may pick fights simply to entertain themselves and fulfill their subconscious need for conflict.

What a generosity to help others!

The Aries sign is a strange combination of selfishness and generosity. Aries people can be self-absorbed and self-centered at times, but this is also one of the most altruistic signs, and Aries people are usually quick to help those in need, even at great personal cost and risk. Tell them you are in danger and you need their help, they are there very fast. This, combined with the Aries propensity to take risks, leads many Aries people into the rescuing professions such as firefighter, paramedic, peacekeeper or coast guard.

Aries people enter politics, to change the system from within. Most Aries people have a strong interest in politics, though this may take the form of argument rather than action, but if their Saturn and Jupiter are good in natal chart, they can be very good administrators and politicians.

- *Always Young, physically, mentally*

- *Aries people tend to be fun, lively, playful and youthful. Many look younger than their chronological ages and most retain some childlike qualities throughout adulthood, both physically and psychologically. When we talk about Youth, strength and fame we think about Skanda, Lord Shanmuga in Indian Puranas, the six headed Warrior who is considered great for six attributes viz. Jnana (wisdom), Vairagya (dispassion), Bala (strength), Kirti (fame), Sree (wealth) and Aishvarya (divine powers). He was born in one of the Aries Nakshtras(moon sign) "Krithiga". In fact he had other combinations to have those six qualities.*

- *Despite the emotional courage of this sign, Aries people are surprisingly sensitive and eager to please. Though they can be pushy and domineering or controlling at times, they are also idealistic, trusting, and in great need of reassurance.*

- *Optimistically go at it*

- *Aries people do nothing in half-measures. Anything they choose to do, they do fully and completely. They are stubborn and generally refuse to accept defeat, even long after a situation has become untenable. They rarely stay down for long though, as this is a naturally optimistic sign that bounces back quickly from misfortune and strife. Aries people have a way of coming out on top in most situations.*

5. WHAT IS RIGHT? WHAT IS WRONG?

23 Aug 09

The whole world and the whole cosmos are working on two basic principles- Zero and one. I am not only talking about binary form of thinking of computers, but also of humans and other living and non living organs also.

I give you a story about evolution from the angle of God believers. It can be different slightly for non-believers of God. Because I see the difference is very, very tiny.

There was only one God who was occupying the whole cosmos. He was totally blissful, happy. Sometime he felt bored to be still. The omni potent created large chess board and the black and white pieces. The chess rules were the same as of today. He started to play from one side and moved the white pieces. The next move he played the black pieces. After some time, he was bored sitting in the same place and moving both pieces. Then he will sit in one side and move white pieces and after that will go to the opposite side and move black pieces, it went on for some time. Here he had a problem. It was not that interesting as when he moved to the black-side, he knew exactly the plan of the white side, as he was both the white and black side player. He thought for a while. He made it a rule as when he moves to the other side, he should forget the plan of the white side and only when he comes back to white he will remember the plan. Same rule applies to black side also. Now it became quite interesting.

There was now the time/space problem of moving every time to the other side. How to avoid that? He thought of it and decided to create a replica of himself, everything alike-no difference. Only difference is one will be thinking everything from one side to make it interesting. He just named the one side as 0 and the other side as 1. This is how the entire cosmos was formed, from 0s and 1s.

How to further the interest? There are more games created. To adjust to the nature of games, different forms and shapes of his being created to enjoy the thrill of play. Now there was a small problem, the different beings are so involved in their form and structure that they forget their origin and the thought that they all are the Supreme Being that can do anything.

To put it simply, this is the basic principle of Advaita. Anything that is right for one being can be wrong for somebody else. People, who are struck with their philosophies, rather than themselves, come back in the later stages of their life to say that they were wrong. All religions, philosophies are created to cater to the needs of difference and then to make us understand from the difference. If there is no understanding of the others, then the whole (Maya) illusion takes care of you. To understand, first step is to realise yourself, YOU, the spark of the Supreme Lord. You can go back as Supreme Lord or struck with tiny little tags attached to your life, which comes from the name, gender, fame, profession, birth, stature, nationality, religion, etc.

THE ENTIRE DECISION IS YOURS.

6. IT IS NOT CLEAR HOW A PERSON (CAPRICORN ASC) CAN **WEAR BLUE SAPPHIRE AND RED CORAL TOGETHER, WHEN THERE IS ENMITY OF MARS WITH THE LAGNA LORD??**

25 Aug 09

This was a question that was asked when I indicated that a native of Asc (lagna) Capricorn wanted to wear both, red coral and blue sapphire.

The basic principle of wearing gems can be categorised broadly into two:

1) To ward off evil of bad planets

2) To enhance the effects of good planets.

Different astrologers have different views about which one is better.

We take the above example Capricorn- for Capricorn Saturn is the lagna lord. Blue Sapphire is considered good to strengthen him. Why would we strengthen him? If he is in good position, by wearing this gem his effects will be strengthened.

What if he is in a bad position? The view is even if he is in bad position he is the lagna lord, everything for the horoscope happens through him.

What if, for the same lagna, the fourth and eleventh house lord Mars is in good position?

Here people argue that Mars is enemical to Saturn; But, what about fourth house and eleventh house lordships? They may not in fact want, Mars to be strength less and deter the fourth house and labh sthana karakathva? All the nine planets need be placed in one of the 12 houses in the horoscope. Enmity of planet is only one of the aspects. We need not confuse that here.

Generally speaking, if Mars is strong, courage, land ownership, leadership by strength will be strong in a horoscope. It doesn't matter whether Mars is enemy or friend to a lagna lord. Whatever the relationship of Jupiter for a lagna, if Jupiter is strong, children, higher positions, long term wealth will be good. Here I emphasise, we are not talking about the lordship of houses. We talk purely about the relationship with lagna lord who can be enemic or friendly.

Red Coral can be worn by the native if Mars is placed in 1, 4, 10, 11th houses.

This will ward of his debts. In combination with Sapphire the lagna lord, this will definitely reduce his debt. Here we need not confuse the enmity anymore.

7.ASTROLOGICAL TRAITS FOR SIMHA RASI OR SIMHA LAGNA (LEO)

Physical Appearance: Leonians have broad shoulders, ruddy or florid complexion, large bones and muscles. Tall, upright upper body better formed than lower. Thin waist, prominent knees, Soft and wavy hair usually light in colour with tendency to baldness, Head full sized and round, Full stature and majestic appearance, imposing, commanding and dignified. Broadly complexion will vary according to their planets in and aspects the Ascendant. He will be tall, well built, catching and large staring eyes. In short a royal disposition.

Mental Tendencies: Ambitious, generous, honourable, frank warm hearted, self confident fearless, impulsive, determined, preserving and conscientious. Fond of power and distinction, liking for art, cheerful, optimistic disposition, magnanimous and generous; large hearted and noble but harsh in   temperament.

Personality : Good natured, philosophical, frank, free and outspoken, strong Willed, independent, forceful and impulsive, inspiring, they have great hope. ' are Helpful to mankind and other creations of God. They hold wise judgment. They always forgive others and forget the mistakes, sins, and errors of others, Very independent in views, have excellent organising powers, they are constructive, inventive, magnanimous and ingenious. They are subject to flattery but do not fall victim to it. Being a fiery sign Leonian are ambitious, hopeful to the last minute, brilliant, boasting clever actions, commanding, domineering, enthusiastic, joyous and full of jubilation. They are good planners, leaders and have vitality and vigour. They are of rash temperament but their outbursts do not last long; brave, constant in love and relations and helpful to everybody. But they are generally teased by opponents and enemies whom they face bravely and with courage and confidence; over liberal and extrovert. They are hasty and become irritated, they arrive at forcing and hasty conclusion and suffer. They have generally robust health. For good health and temperate living and balanced diet is absolutely necessary for them..

Health and Disease: Leonians generally keep a good and splendid health. In case they fall ill, they tend to recover rapidly from any illness. But they are easily alarmed whenever sickness overtakes them. Leo indicates heart, the spinal column, column, spinal marrow, nerves, fiber, bone, intestinal muscles, anterior and posterior coronary.

So heart disease, palpitation of heart, spinal meningitis, sun stroke, giddiness, inflammations, epilepsy, and rheumatic fever are the diseases indicated for this sign. When Aquarius and Capricorn with afflicted or positioned with malefic planets, it may cause swelling the ankle followed by heart disease. Jupiter in Leo or aspect Leo will protect one from surgical operation etc. but if Mars afflicts Leo it will indicate surgical operations etc.

So in order to keep good health and particularly to avoid heart affliction one should take balanced diet, avoid drinks, stimulants and beverages etc. In other words Leonians should have Sattvic diet.

Finance and Fortune: Leonians are generally fortunate and have sufficient resources. They are spendthrifts; their bank position may be deteriorating as age advances. They are tempted to gambling and speculation but they are luckily rewarded, they should avoid this. As they are liberal and do not hesitate to assist anybody, rather feel proud and pleasure past them at a loss and in trouble in old age, so they should control this habit.

Leonians often occupy a position of trust and authority. They try to deal with large issues and leave the minor details to their subordinates. Actually they are born rulers. They should save for the old age due to the fact that their lavish spending nature may face financial troubles as age advances from youth   onwards.

Romance, Marriage and Married Life: Leonians are romantic, ideal lovers, fiery in passions but sincere and faithful in love. But they will not show any demonstration of love in public as they consider it below their dignity.

Leonian will have great affection to the opposite sex and remain in the crowd of ladies, so the partner should not be jealous of them but have proper understanding rather than doubting each other. They maintain harmony in domestic life unless the 7th house or lord thereof is afflicted, then there will be bickering between the partners. They will love their children most, and feel very proud of them. Children will be of independent views, dislike restrictions and may become nervous and restless. So Leo people should rely on their children otherwise they may loose their confidence. Their children will be good organisers, not arrogant, popular, good natured, obliging and affectionate also courageous and confident if they are also born in Leo. But this does not mean that children born in other signs will not have upper qualities, their characteristic will be governed by the sign in which they are born.

Male Spouse: Leonian husbands are exciting, love their wives extremely but are centre of attractions for other ladies. If his wife understands Leo husband and agrees with him, then she will be liked, admired and loved. Such people fit in the domestic routine, admirably; they will never allow any body to disrespect their spouse or any member of his family. They cannot tolerate ill repute. They are always conscious of their social standing and are chivalrous. They are passionate and of loving nature but rash in temperament. So, it is advised to Leo born that couple should understand each other to make the home happy and fortunate.

Female Spouse: Such ladies are ambitious and ideal. They manage their home ideally, are successful social worker and make favourable impressions on all. She will command social and prominent position is a self sacrificing and has an everlasting love.

A Leo born lady need not doubt her Leo born husband for being popular in opposite sex, not selfish and does not expect return from others for having done good to them. Leo born ladies need one to keep her under control so that she can appreciate her husband's good nature, affection, kindness and real love to lead a pleasant, prosperous and peaceful life. They are very passionate and require self sex control lest they go beyond limits, are of fixed ideas, dogmatic views and expect that their word should be law in the home.

Of a Male born in Leo sign marries a Leo born girl will create a problem for him to please her for her dress and jewellery etc. If he does not satisfy her in life it will be Hell. But if he is able to meet her demands, the home is then Heaven with more compatibility.

Ideal Match: Leo is a fiery sign and is best suited for Aries and Sagittarius other two fiery signs and the three Airy signs, Gemini, Libra or Aquarius born people for more compatibility.

Aries and Sagittarius born will contribute full happiness and harmony. Aquarius born are devoted to Leo, Libra born will ever try for company, avoid troubles and purchase peace at any cost and time. One born in Gemini will be very tactful, inseparable, sincere and affectionate. One always tries to please the partner.

A Leo bride marrying Aries husband is lucky, as she has a commanding person so that she will know her limits and will not overstep in exercising her authority or spending lavishly.

Domestic Environments : Since Leonians are born to rule, so they will try to be leader in the house and expect all those in home to be submissive, cooperative, obedient and grateful to him. They like the family members to be magnanimous and noble. They try to keep peace, harmony and happiness all these will keep him cheerful. The health needs relaxation. They will keep home tidy, decorative and attractive. They are Careful and choosy for dress, furniture, curtains etc.

They are very choosy for their friends, and entertain them often. They never hesitate to spend money to keep their prestige and honour, not economical even in the state of poverty. They will lead an aristocratic life and their home will be an impressive one.

Professions: Leo born people are famous and high positioned in commerce or in government. They will have fixed income, security of job, and it gives executive ability and tireless working capacity. One will be best suited as manager of the big concerns, corporation or director, captain, sales manager   etc.

Planets forming favourable aspects specify the   nature   of   profession.

Traits to be corrected: Since Leonians are determined and of dogmatic views they should take other's views, ideas and suggestions before deciding any issue. Leonians are extroverts, roar like a lion and get into trouble, which temperament should be avoided, especially during the sub period of the evil planet which afflicts Sun, any argumentative nature, altercations and actions annoying superiors be avoided, they should not be hasty and get irritated.

Leonians should avoid forcing their desires and opinions on others, should be never arrogant, restrict their wants, should take lessons from the past, behave in an attractive manner, be economical for the old age and maintain bank position. Avoid rash temperament and impulsiveness. Be patient, careful do not be carried away by others, flattery and on top of all they should remain more detached from feelings.

Lucky Days, Colours, Numbers and Stones : Sundays, Tuesday, Wednesday, Thursday and Friday are favourable days whereas Monday, Saturdays of the week be avoided for important works and staring new ventures.

The numbers 1,4,5,9 and 6 are lucky; avoid 2, 7 and 8 whereas passive number is 3. Colours are Orange, Red and Green. Avoid Blue, White and Black.

Ruby or Emerald in gold is to be used in 3rd finger of right hand on Sunday morning after prayers. When Sun is afflicted, unfavourable or in fall, one should use Ruby plus Red Coral or Ruby plus Emerald in Gold.

Fasting: To reduce the evils, keep fast on full Moon days regularly throughout your life.

8.Maha Dasa Traits (Main Period) Rahu:

In Indian Vedic astrology, the Rahu is associated with being religious. Therefore, in favourable time, the bearer or native may make profits from the establishment / government or employer or else alike through a person of different religion. Rahu is also associated with expansion, especially of kingdom, religion, higher knowledge and going on pilgrimage. Traveling is also associated. It influences one's mind and gives nervousness or frees from worries if it is auspicious. It is also associated with litigation. If auspicious, brings victory.

In our opinion, the native can wear "Gomed (Sardonyx) / Hessonite" of Gaya or Ceylon or chant regularly the Mantra of Rahu to get the good and auspicious results enhanced and more favourable. The weight of Gomed can be decided as one Ratti for every 10 Kg. of body weight of the native and worn on any Saturday in night in the Large (Middle) Finger. This act is likely to appease Rahu.

9. LIZARDS FALLING ON RIGHT HAND

If lizard falls on right hand wrist what will happen? Anonymous, India

Answer: Generally for male if lizard falls on wrist some beautification/modification will happen. For complete Male/Female body part chart see here.

பல்லி தோஷம் by R.S.

It is a general dosha chart if Lizard falls or pass through these body parts.

Lizard Dosha

Lizard Falling Effect on Men	
Head	Be ready for disputes / Clashes
Top head	Afraid of death
Face	Expect financial profits
Left eye	It's for good
Right eye	Un-successful / Fail / Lost
Forehead	Lack of involvement / Separation
Right cheek	Sadness
Left ear	Beneficial / Income
Upper Lip	Be ready for disputes
Lower Lip	Expect financial profits
Both lips together	Fear of death
Mouth	Fear of bad health condition
Left of the backside	Victory / Gain

Night dreams	Fear of king or Ruler
Wrist	Beautification / Modification
Arm	Financial loss / Failure
Fingers	Expect visitors and old friends
Right arm	Trouble / Complexity
Left arm	May bring shame on you
Thighs	Loss of clothing
Mustache	Expect hurdles
Back foot	Get ready for a journey
Toes	Physical illness

Lizard Falling Effect on Women	
Head	Afraid of death
Hair Knot	Worry about sickness
Calf of the leg	Expect visitors
Left eye	Get love from your man
Right eye	Creates mental stress
Chest	It's for good
Right cheek	Male child may born
Upper Right ear	Expect financial profits
Upper lip	Be ready for disputes
Lower lip	You'll get new things

Both lips together	Ready to face difficulties
Breast	Unhappiness may occur
Backside	Expect death news
Nails	Conflicts / Arguments
Hands	Expect financial profits
Left arm	Creates mental stress
Fingers	Get ornaments
Right arm	Romance ahead
Shoulders	Getting ornaments
Thighs	Expect romance
Knees	Fondness / Affection

Ankle	Complexity / Trouble
Right leg	You will be defeated / Loss
Toes	Male child may born

10. MALAYALAM, TAMIL, SAKA, GEORGIAN MONTHS

Comparative table showing corresponding months of other calendars

The months are named after the constellations of the zodiac. Thus Chingam (from *Simham* or Lion) is named after the constellation Leo and so on. The following are the months of the astronomical Malayalam calendar:

Months in Malayalam Era	In Malayalam	Gregorian Calendar	Tamil calendar	Saka era
Chingam	⮚ ിങ്ങം	August-September	Aavani - Purattasi	Sravan-Bhadrapada
Kanni	കന്നി	September-October	Purattasi-Aippasi	Bhadrapada - Asvina
Thulam	∎ ⟩⧠ ⊃ം	October-November	Aippasi - Karthigai	Asvina - Kartika
Vrishchikam	∎ ⟩ശ്ചി കം	November-December	Karthigai - Margazhi	Kartika - Agrahayana
Dhanu	ധനു	December-January	Margazhi - Thai	Agrahayana - Pausa

Makaram	കരം	January - February	Thai - Maasi	Pausa - Magha
Kumbha m	കുംഭ ം	February-March	Maasi - Panguni	Magha - Phalguna
Meenam	ീനം	March-April	Panguni - Chithtrai	Phalguna - Chaitra
Medam	േ ം	April-May	Chithtrai - Vaikasi	Chaitra - Vaisakha
Edavam	ഏടവ ം	May-June	Vaikasi- Aani	Vaisakha - Jyaistha
Midhuna m	ിഥുനം	June-July	Aani - Aadi	Jyaistha - Asada
Karkadak	കർക്കട	July-	Aadi -	Asada -

QUESTION AND ANSWERS

1. IN-LAW HEALTH PROBLEMS AND CFA EXAMS:

Question:

Date of Birth: 13-10-1974
Time of Birth: 7:40PM
Place of Birth: Madurai
Gender: Male

Please give me a brief of my husband's horoscope. His parents are always complaining of ill health, can u tell me based on his horoscope what remedies we can do. Will we settle down permanently in USA? Also he has his CFA level 1 exam this June, please tell me how successful will he be. My info is 28th March 1981 at 7:45AM Chennai, even I am giving CFA level1, Will I be successful in the exam.

From: -- Anonymous United States
Date: **01/06/10**

Charting I have done through Vedicschoalar

Answer:

Hi, Parents ill health: When their horoscope is not available - we examine the fourth house, (from lagna and rasi) and ninth house (from lagna and rasi), fourth and sixth from fourth house for mother's health; fourth and sixth from ninth house for father- their strength in the horoscope, Sun and moon in general for the karkathvam, dasa bhukthi as well as the current transitory positions. Lagna karaka Mars (he is the eight house lord also) himself is in 6th house with 4th house lord moon and sun with debilitated Venus. The 11th house has retrograde Jupiter. Rahu in lagna karaka Mars's another house being the eighth from lagna He is running

Pisces	Aries	Taurus	Gemini
	Asc	**Ketu**	**Sat**
Aquarius	13-10-1974		Cancer
Jup	19.40 Madurai		
Capricorn	**9n56, 78e07**		Leo
	Rasi		
Sagittarius	Scorpio	Libra	Virgo
	Rahu	**Mer**	**Sun**
			Moon
			Ven
			Mars

Rahu Dasa Venus (deb) Antara. The next three antaras are Sun, Moon and Mars-all in sixth house. Short/medium term respite has already started at least for father from the Saturn's transit in Sept, 2009-(from 12 Saturn was seeing ninth for 2 1/2 years. Please do Sani and Rahu Preethi.

- Yes you will do better in foreign country, especially west (Rahu(eight-indicates period outside- eight is always out of comfort zone, Jupiter the ninth house lord (for long term settlement in foreign)in labh sthana indicates profitability in foreign , Saturn –the lord of 10 and 11 in upaya sthana positions assert that) - but there will be obstacles that you need to surmount in Rahu Dasa.

- For his father and mother also, it is good if he stays away from them.

- But mind you most of his gains, fame, possessions arise from his father and mother's strength in horoscope. Therefore, pl. take care of them and get their aasirvatham, which forms the basis of everything in his horoscope.

- His examination, he needs to work very hard because of Sade satti, but success achievable based on overall strength of horoscope.

Pisces **Sun** **Ven** **Mars**	Aries **Asc**	Taurus	Gemini
Aquarius **Mer**	28th March 1981 at 7:45AM Chennai **13n05**, **80e17** **Rasi** Sun Dasha and Ketu Antardasha.		Cancer **Rahu**
Capricorn **Ketu**			Leo
Sagittarius **Moon**	Scorpio	Libra	Virgo **Jup** **Sat**

- For you, the running Sun Dasha and Ketu antara - sun (5th house lord- aspected by Jupiter and Saturn) and Ketu (aspected by Jupiter) from 10th house) dasa,antara and other planetary positions indicate, it can be a cake walk for you, but keep it with you and encourage your husband for a joint study. Get away the Sagittarius and Virgo-inferiority, superiority traits, both of you are unique in different aspects, he knows the knack of doing things, you are as straight as a line.

Note for students: For higher education fifthhouse and for Specialisation desired, the strength of the karaka planets for that specialisation be considered. If it is just the degree then fourth house need to be analysed in conjunction with 2nd and fifth. Here fifth house lord is fourth to moon sign and his dasa is running , for CFA – Sun Venus and Mercury need to be taken into account- Here you see Mercury has got 11th house, Venus is exalted and in fourth from moon. Sun and Venus are with lagna lord aspected by **"Jupiter"** (I take it with 25% discount for the compound relationship with lagna lord) and the lord of tenth and eleventh house- Saturn. The antara planet is in ten seeing fourth house indicating career related efforts.

Date: **01/06/10**

2. SOFTWARE JOB DEMANDING AND NO PEACE OF MIND:

Question:

Hi, this question is regarding guidance in my career. I am working in a software technology company in US. My current job responsibilities are more and demanding when compared to my position and salary, with less peace of mind. I would like to know if this is a good time to go for change in job or career path or when my career situation will be good in terms of good rise and promotion and especially w.r.t peace of mind as well. Do I have a chance to start something of my own at any point of my career? Please advice on my career situation.

Date of Birth: 02-05-1974
Birth Time: 8:20 AM
Birth Place: Ongole, Andhra Pradesh, India
Gender: Male
From: Anonymous California US
Date: **01/03/10**

Pisces Ven	Aries Sun Mer	Taurus Asc Ketu	Gemini Mars Sat
Aquarius Jup	02-05-1974 8.20 a.m. Ongole 15n31, 80e04 Rasi		Cancer
Capricorn			Leo Moon
Sagittarius	Scorpio Rahu	Libra	Virgo

Answer:

You are Leo in Vedic Astrology (Moon sign). Your lagna is Vrishaba. You are running Rahu Dasa from your seventh house. Mercury Buddhi. (Mercury the 2nd and fifth house lord is in viraya sthana 12) That is one of the reasons for your problem from superiors and inadequate financial compensation for your work. When Rahu Dasa Ketu Buddhi stars on2011-02-13 ~ 01:44 this will change. The next thing we should see is the strength of your lagna lord and lagna. Your Lagna lord is Venus. He is exalted (Uchcha) in eleventh house Pisces 3-28-53(Labh - profit sthana). So position and strength are very good. He is in Uttarabhadrapada (Saturn nakshatra)-. Saturn being your 9th and tenth house lord and Poorna Yogakaraka, he is in extremely beneficial-nakshatra. But your lagna is occupied by Ketu; your dasa karaka Rahu is aspecting your lagna from 7th house. For your horoscope I will give 75% marks.

Pisces	Aries	Taurus	Gemini **Ketu**
Aquarius **Jup**	*Transit Chart On 02.01.2010*		Cancer **Moon** **Mars**
Capricorn			Leo **Asc**
Sagittarius **Sun** **Mer** **Ven** **Rahu**	Scorpio	Libra	Virgo **Sat**

• Coming to the transitory positions, you are under the last phase of the 7

1/2 years of Saturn transit (12th, 1st and 2nd) - Recently Saturn went to your second house. Before that from your Janma lagana he saw your tenth house (job house) that was the reason for all your discomforts in the last 2 1/2 years. In your chart. Guru is in tenth house(job house) and tenth house lord Saturn(your job house lord) is in second house with seventh and twelfth house lord mars(mars not strong)Moon aspects Tenth house and Jupiter. Guru - Saturn Moon and Mars combination makes you think in other lines. But your profit/cash flow is related to IT industry because of Venus. Most of your work involves sweet talk- don't leave it under any pressure. If you start another business in addition, then there are reasons for it coming good in few years. But don't leave job to start a business. The fourth house lord (business) house is occupied by Moon aspected by Jupiter. I don't see any problem starting a business, but I see both possibilities combined together.

• Your job front problems will vanish this year, but slowly one by one. Your efforts for promotion and increment will fructify at the end of this year. Please see the attached document for general nature of your Rasi and Rahu Dasa

3. SON WAS CHEATED INTO MARRIAGE WITH HEART PROBLEM GIRL:

Question:

He got married and there was the finding of depression conditions and congenital heart problems in the girl and the marriage was nullified? What was the reason? When will he be married again? My particulars; Lady- - DOB 02-12-1959 TOB: 18.50 hours Trichi, INDIA: 10n49, 78e41, My son was born in 1984. But I want you to check from my horoscope rather

From: -- Anonymous Unknown
Date: **12/30/09**

Answer:

Dear Madam, I have checked your horoscope, you were born in Mithuna Lagna and Dhanur Rasi. Poorvada Nakshatra. You are running Rahu Maha Dasa and Venus Antara. Ketu is in your Fourth house and Venus is in your 5th house in Mooltrikona. Your fifth house and ninth house need to be studied to find out the problem of your son. As mentioned above your fifth house Lord Venus sitting in his own house which happens to be Mooltrikona sthana. Your children will be kind and helpful to you in all respects. They will bring glory to your family. The one important note you should remember is, as your Buddhi Sthana is also 5th house, you always think about your children and sometimes you may lose focus on vital factors like not being sitting as a friend and guide to them rather you act just too kind to them and not controlling them towards their own goals. Venus aspecting your labh sthana tells me that you will benefit quite a lot from your children and will lead a very happy life through them.

Pisces **Ketu**	Aries	Taurus	Gemini **Asc**
Aquarius	02-12-1959 18.50 hours Trichi, 10n49, 78e41 Rasi		Cancer
Capricorn			Leo
Sagittarius **Moon** **Sat**	Scorpio **Sun** **Mer** **Mars** **Jup**	Libra **Ven**	Virgo **Rahu**

Your fourth house Rahu is running your dasa, normally Kanya Rahu is bound to bring bounties in your family. Four other planets are in your 6th house. They are Sun, Mercury, Mars and Jupiter. You might have heard about 6th house. When important planets sit there they try to present you problems and the strong Mars in association with Jupiter and your Lagna Karaka Mercury and your Dairya sthanathipathi Sun are solving those problems. So you are bound to face enemies and difficulties and you will solve them by your courageous actions. Your seventh house is hosting Saturn (eighth house and ninth house lord) and dhana sthanathipathi Moon.

The problem of your son is only transitory given your strong horoscope strengthening your children.

When we don't have horoscope we have some other way of doing it. When you have strong Venus as fifth house lord, usually he should also have strength in his Venus. When your 9th house lord (another sthana to see your son) Saturn is strong, his Saturn should also be somehow strong. I see these two planets association. Moon is with Saturn. I think his moon will also be strong somehow. So I get three strong planets here that of Saturn, Moon and Venus. Saturn is ayulkaraka. Strong Saturn says your son has long life as well as his proper would be wife will have longevity of life. When Venus is good, it indicates good married life. Therefore I can presume the problems so far are just trivial and his real life would be a strong happy married life. Strong moon is indicative of his association with mother.

When your Rahu and Venus dasa bhukthi are running definite marriage of your son is indicated. Saturn moving from 9th house to 10th in transition is also better for your son's prospects. Jupiter is seeing the 9th house from 3. All indications are for him to marry between now and July, 2010.

If you have any other query please feel free to ask. I have given you 1 free question

4. TRANSIT EFFECTS OF JUPITER IN KUMBHA FOR MY CAREER:

Question:

Really I am very grateful to your overwhelming support during my bad time. My job search is in progress and I hope with your blessings I will get one very soon. Mean while Jupiter is transiting to Kumbha on 19th December. How this transit and what is are its effects on my chart? Any significant developments are indicated. DOB:-05th July 1977 Birth time:-20:23pm

Birth Place:-Miraj, Maharashtra, India
From: Anonymous- Muscat, UAE
Date: **12/04/09**

Answer:

Dear SKr, You have all our blessings for the best things to come in your life.

As I explained earlier I take your Rasi Aquarius for transitions. Jupiter is not that good in twelfth house. In the one year he was in Makara your twelfth house from Rasi, it created lot of expenditure in anything you can think of. Your thinking power was somehow blunted and you could not take decisions. You were unable to sleep for usual hours. Many of your efforts were thwarted by unexpected events. Wife side temporal incompatibility was there in the day and night. Relations and children brought only expenditure after expenditure. You had anger on your side when dealing with anything.

Now, although first house transition of Jupiter is not considered auspicious, the above mentioned problems are improving from 19th Dec onwards for you.

With Jupiter's seventh house aspect, your friends, wife will be sweet to take care of you. A small/medium winning in lottery like things is possible. Your Gurus, uncles, bosses will be friendlier than in the last one year. Your children will progress in education and will behave well with you. With ninth house aspect you will travel to holy places and meet holy people. Your job search may be fruitful because of Jupiter seeing your fifth and ninth houses as your horoscope is good. Normally when Jupiter is in first house there will be fluidity in everything in your life. Nothing will look like concise or concrete. Even when you get a new job the acclimatisation will take longer and you may feel that your previous one was better - but that is only an illusion because of Rasi Jupiter.

Take the scenarios 1) Interview time: When everything goes well there will be some irritating events or questions that may put you off for the job - but be patient it is just because of the Rasi Jupiter - Try to please people(keep your distance as well) and get that job- the ball is in your court. 2) Selection time: When you get a call informing your selection, there will be questions about salary or placement in a different position or place. Never mind- change is always happening; you are part of the process. 3) Got the job: Please be sure you relate to people in a business-like manner, never try to under-react or overreact to events happening in the new office.

What will happen when the next transit of Jupiter happens in approximately one year? Jupiter in second is auspicious. Money matters will improve. Promotions, change of job for better will happen. You will bear sweet words. Family will be the happiest lot in your surroundings. Blessings again

Date: **12/07/09**

5. RAHU KETU TRANSIT WHEN WILL THEY GIVE EFFECT WHEN ENTERING OR AFTER HALF PERIOD SPENT:

Question:

DOB:-05th July 1977 Birth time:-20:23pm Birth Place: Miraj, Maharashtra, India. Let me know the Rahu and Ketu transit to (Dhanu and Mithuna) effects on me? Check the effects from Natal moon, Arudha Lagna and Lagna. To see transit effects which is the correct position natal moon, AL or lagna? While transiting when they will give results I mean when they enter sign or when they spend half period in a sign or during leaving the sign? Which one will be most helpful for me during this transit and why you think so?

From: Anonymous- Sharjahi, UAE
Date: **11/09/09**

Answer:

When one of my gurus Dr.C.S.Seshadri was a direct disciple of K.P. he asked the same question. To calculate transitory position of Rahu, Ketu, Saturn and Jupiter which is to be taken into account- Lagna or Moon sign? K.P. said up to middle age around 35-40 years (at that time) Moon sign and after that Lagna. But he gave exceptions, if the lagna and lagna lord are feeble, then Moon Sign takes precedence, same way if the rashi and rashi lord are feeble then always Lagna. Your Lagna is stronger of the two- as aspected by Jupiter as well as lagna lord and lagna lord in kendra. But still I would consider Raashi Aquarius as you are still under 40-45(change because of changed life expectancy). Raashi is not feeble as a varghothamam takes place between moon and Saturn they change places- this is strong enough. Rahu and Ketu according one ephemeris are transiting houses on November 17, 2009. Rahu is transiting from Capricorn into Sagittarius, while Ketu is moving from Cancer into Gemini where they will remain for the next 18 months.

For Aquarians, Rahu and Ketu act like Saturn and Mars in more respects.

Some of your debt problems were associated with transitory Rahu in twelfth house, creating havoc of expenditures and debts. Your sleep, bed-side happiness was somewhat extinct for the last 18 months. Now that he moved to eleventh house you can expect 1) cut in wasteful expenditure, immediately. 2) You will sleep normally, and bed-side pleasure is back again.

11th house Rahu is bound to bring plenty of unexpected windfalls, Long journeys which will be joyful, your elder brother/sister or people you consider in those positions will be helpful and you will help them. There will be ways found to earn that extra income.

From 6th house Ketu made you interact with learned people and astrologers and he kindled your enthusiasm towards spiritual matters. Now that he moves to 5th, your mind will be in oscillation most of the time. Children and maternal relations will bring some stress in your life. Your ancestral possessions will have some kind of problems. You could create some rifts with your managers, therefore please be careful, in talking to them.

Overall financially the next 18 months will be better off than the last 18.

Date: **11/08/09**

6.   WHEN WILL I GET MARRIED?
Question:

D.O.B.: 07-04-1984, born Madras probably at 3.40 a.m I am not sure about the time although they say the lagna is Kumbha. Can you tell me more about my would-be wife and when will I get married.
From: -- Anonymous Unknown
Date: **10/24/09**

Answer:

Hi dear, Thanks for choosing me to shoot your very important question in life that of your spouse. You have not given your name to reverse engineer your time of birth.O.K. just find out So I now do sputam to find out the possibility of male in that lagna on that day. What is sputam? Jataka Phala Chintamani is quoted as below:

Analambvagni Bhoovyoma Jala Vayvadhipaha. Khagaha II

Kramatharkadayo Vare Swaswakala Pravarthakaha II

Bhoomyadi Pada Ghatika Vriddhisyadardha Yamake Yamottarardhe Thadhrasatharohakshavarohanam Rohanam II

Parivrittidwayam Yame Prathi Praharameedrisam II

Sthree Janma Jala Vayvosyadbhoonabhognishu. Pum Janihi II

Ethena Ghatika Gyanam Thena Lagnam Vinir. Disheth II

For finding male born in the lagna I use this 5 Tatwa theory and get your birth time in Kumbha lagna and segregate it for male birth timings. The time mentioned by you 3.40 is rightlyfalling into it and it is Kumbha lagna. So it is confirmed for our purposes. Now,you have Kumbha Lagna and Rishaba Rasi - Mrigasirsha Nakshatra. You are running your Jupiter Dasa. Here is your horoscope.

Pisces **Sun** **Ven**	Aries **Mer**	Taurus **Moon** **Rahu**	Gemini
Aquarius **Asc**	Seventh ap eighty four 3.40 **13n05, 80e17** **Rasi**		Cancer
Capricorn			Leo
Sagittarius **Jup**	Scorpio **Mars** **Ketu**	Libra **Sat**	Virgo

To see your wife's bhala - first we look at your seventh house. Seventh house lord Sun is placed with exalted Venus in Second house. Seventh house is aspected by Jupiter (your dasa lord- second and eleventh house lord). In your suha sthana Rahu is with your 6th house lord Moon. You just finished your rahu Dasa in the few months before.

When talking to you I understand that you already had a break or divorce. This should have happened in Rahu Dasa (Rahu in Rohini 2, taking over Moon's job) Chandra Bhukthi (He gave away his full powers of sixth house to Rahu to disturb you and when the antara of Rahu was there in moon bhukthi – all enemies join to pull you down- this should have been arranged and marriage itself would have performed in Rahu-Moon-Jupiter as Jupiter is second house lord.

When you ask about your wife, I can say you mean the second wife. Eleventh house is the house for second wife. Eleventh house lord Jupiter is sitting in his own house and running his dasa. If Jupiter alone is there I would have said differently, but when he is aspected by your Lagna and twelfth house lord Saturn I would say your 2nd wife would be very fair to fair, medium height and lean to medium weight, Seeing your second house and where the Jupiter drishti is, then I can say she will be from very respected family connected either with powerful politics or film industry or very rich business family. She will be great achiever herself, dynamic and she will be good companion for you.

Your marriage will take place from April, 2010 to end of that year. Jupiter-Saturn starts from 25-3-2010. Jupiter is on Purvashada-2 on your Poorna Yogakaraka (Venus) Patha. Your lagna and bed suha sthana lord Saturn is aspecting him from your best of all places in a chart that of 9th house . Saturn is exalted there. He is in Visaka 1 that is Jupiter pada (Jupiter your 2nd and 11th house lord- 11th house is for second wife)

Your married life will be very affluent with lot of wealth. The marriage will last forever. You will have good two boys and a girl as blessed children.

Date: **10/25/09**

7.   BUSINESS CHANGE AND PROFIT:
Question:

Date of Birth: 22-08-85
Time of Birth: 6:00 AM
Place of Birth: Baroda, Gujarat
Gender: Male

Jai Shree Krishna. My birth information is as follows: DOB: August 22nd, 1985 Time: 6 AM Place: Baroda (Vadodara, Gujarat, India) I have been in US from past 6 years. I came to US to study but don't know how I got involved in business. Currently, I am involved in Oil & Retail business which is going alright but I am really not satisfied as I keep feeling like I should do bigger business. So I have been trying to sell my business but every time somebody comes to buy it; something goes wrong even after having a highly profitable business. When will I be able to sell my business and move into something bigger? I want to ask about my marriage as I am having difficulty getting married as some problems comes... When will I be able to get married? Can you please tell me something about my wife?? .. How will be my married life? How will be my wife by nature and looks? I have a dream of building a solar power plant and start a public traded company to raise money after investing some of my own ... would I be able to ever build one? In my chart I have Shani, ketu & moon in thula rashi .. I know that Shani with ketu doesn't do badly, but I read somewhere that Shani and Chandra together are bad... How bad is it? Actually I have found out that it gives u mental instability... which i suffer from ... I had a speech problem but after praying everyday of my life...Somehow God blessed me .. But I have lived all my life in depression and I still do. When will I be mentally stable? I have surya in lagna aspecting my 7th house... is my sun strong? Will it affect my marriage life negatively? I also have a question about my Rahu and Ketu... is my rahu and ketu strong? I have heard that Rahu in 9th destroys luck but I also read that rahu aspecting Kendra with exalted Saturn in 3rd is a raja yoga... can you please explain? When will I see real progress in my career? Will be able to make money through real estate, dance club and alcohol?

Answer:

Blessings. Jai Krishna. I give pointed answers.

First about the strength of your chart - When Lagna karaka sits in lagna - it is considered good. In your case Sun being your lagna karaka in Leo is very good for general direction of the native.

Leo is independent thinking lagna. Sun there makes you think like a king or a minister- Sun is aspecting seventh house-(the only problem is your seventh house lord happened to be Saturn who is not so modern thinker- The seventh house karakathvam of friends, would be spouse,all will support very old established path- that is where your mental worries come from- it is not real it is because of others who impose those things on you). Go in the path you decide, dont care about others heckles.

Pisces	Aries **Rahu**	Taurus	Gemini **Ven**
Aquarius	22-8-1985 6 A.M. **22n18, 73e12**		Cancer **Mer** **Mars**
Capricorn **Jup**			Leo **Asc** **Sun**
Sagittarius	Scorpio	Libra **Moon** **Sat** **Ketu**	Virgo

1) For business we now see your fourth house- The lord of the house Mars is in viraya sthana (12th house)- but he is in neecha avastha- When a planet is in neecha sthana he is unable to take up any positional good or bad related to that house. Therefore I consider Mars is neutral and combined with your dhana and labh sthanathipathi Mercury he can bring some benefits in Business.

2) When you started business your Saturn Dasa /Bhukthi was taking you to that. Most astrologers will agree that Saturn is related to Oil and its people-centric activity of Retail.Saturn being the lord of six and seven in three (uchcha)association with twelfth house(viraya sthana) lord moon and Ketu- I can say you will win things with sustained courage and effort.

3) Jupiter(fifth and 8th house lord) in neecha in 6th house is the reason for your mental dissatisfaction. But he aspects 10th, 12th and second houses. Therefore, you will succeed financially in all endeavours you undertake, whether it is mentally satisfying or not.

4) You are running Saturn and Venus dasa bhukthi. When Venus dasa or antara is running native will think about any business related to Dance club, Alcohol, Easy money making ways, something related to other gender. That is the thinking coming to you now. For the question whether it will be good for you- I will say yes till November, 2011- Selling your company and starting Public limited company can be done now- but with lot of difficulties, but with success.After that when Sun Bukthi comes, your interest will be that of Solar power, will surely pursue and you prove it to be successful if everything done before November, 2012.

5) I dont think Sun aspecting 7th house is a problem, but Saturn with Moon and ketu delays your marriage - You will sure marry a lady whom plead for your help and sympathy. She will be somewhat moody for the combination of Moon. Very fair as Ketu and Moon can change Saturn's black gift and sun's drishti also will change that. She will be lean at marriage(taking Sun's aspect) but will add some weight later on

because of Moon and Ketu(Jal grahass)

6) When your lagna lord is good and ninth house lord is in association with dhana and labh sthana lords, aspected by Jupiter your Overall horoscope is very good to best On a scale of 1 to 9 I will put you into 6.5 to 7

Date: **10/22/09**

8. LOT OF STRESS, CAN I EXPECT A CHANGE OF MAHADASA NEARBY?

Question:

There has been a lot of stress (work or other incidents) that has been eating me lately (especially in the past year) which does not reflect my usual self. There is a lot of uncertainty regarding my current immigration/job situation (which I guess is a very common thing nowadays) but still somehow now I seemed to be stressed by these (unlike my usual nature). Also, I am getting married this year amid all these uncertainties. I was wondering if I could get a detailed analysis of my chart. (current & future). I was wondering if I should try to stick to this job and current situation or move back to India and start over again. Especially I'd like to know if there is a mahadasha change around the corner and the impact if any. I was also wondering how my future life in terms of job and finance would look like. Also how my family life would look like (would it be stress free or would it have its own share of problems). If there are any yogas that indicate any thing that stands out etc... I again would like to thank anyone who took time reading this. Thanks, DOB: 17-Sep-1980 Time: 10:34 PM Place: Thrissur, Kerala, India

From: -- Jane Pittsburgh, PA, USA
Date: **10/17/09**

Answer:

Hi, you have Sun Dasa Saturn antara dasa running from January, 2009. In your chart Sun, Mercury and Saturn are combined in the 5th house. Fifth house being responsible for intellect, superiors/bosses, Government-immigration in your case, gurus, children, higher education, these things would have suffered. Generally Govt Karaka sun in fifth house is considered

Karako Bhava nasthi- But with two other planets this has neutralised to an extent.

Previous to this bhukthi there was Sun Jupiter antara from April, 2008 - Jupiter being eighth house lord in fourth house and twelfth to Dasa lord brought all problems in Suha sthana and untold miseries of eighth house karakathva.

Looking forward, from December,2009 you will have Sun mercury antara- it may not be extremely different because of the conjunctions, but still there will be solutions presented in Job/Immigration matters, since he is the lord of the fifth house, he is in fifth with your Fourth house lord. In Virgo Mercury is exalted that adds to the positive argument. Till November, 2010 try everything about these matters, even financial liquidity and lotto chances are possible.

Pisces	Aries	Taurus Asc	Gemini
Aquarius	17-10-1980 10.34 p.m.		Cancer Ven Rahu
Capricorn Ketu			Leo Jup
Sagittarius Moon	Scorpio	Libra Mars	Virgo Sun Mer Sat

In transit Saturn in 10th is delaying any work that you normally finish. Saturn turns retrograde on 13 Jan 2010 and till 30th May he is retrograde - at this time your Mercury Antara is running- Try everything, during that period, you will succeed.

The next Maha dasa change is in March, 2012 - to Moon

Moon - third house lord in eighth house - is not bad as he is having Jupiter drishti- to see further I look at which nakshatra he is. It is Moola- Further I need to see where Ketu is - Ketu is in ninth - so I would say in Moon dasa you will have backend money coming in and you will be alternating between local/foreign countries for your advantage. (Moon positioning Sagittarius is in upaya-alternation-- Ketu the star in which he is, is in Capricorn Chara rasi- ninth house indicates longer foreign stay and eighth house indicates some fluidity)

Date: **10/21/09**

9.   MENTALLY DISTURBED:

Question:

Date of Birth: 26-01-55
Time of Birth: 18:58
Place of Birth: Chennai, India
Gender: Female

Dear Learned Astrologers My pranaams to all of you. I have a question regarding my health. Since February 2009, I have had some small health ailments, though not very serious continues to bother me all the time. Also, because of my son's career uncertainty, since February till present, I have been mentally disturbed. My health (physically & mentally) all these years has been fairly stable. Can you please let me know what the afflictions are and when things are likely to improve?

Thanks DOB: 26th January 1955 Place: Chennai, India Time: 18:58 pm

From: -- Anonymous Unknown
Date: **10/18/09**

Answer:

Hi, you are running Mercury dasa and Rahu antara. Rahu is in your sixth house. In Sagittarius he is considered in debilitation. Rahu Bhukthi started in December, 2008 from that you would have some kind of small ailments. Whatever said, there are few things that will guard you against anything. Jupiter in Lagna Cancer in exhalted position and Saturn in fourth house (exalted) as well. You are a philosophical guru to many people in your circle. You are disposed sympathetically towards poor and needy. These qualities guard you against anything else. Sixth house Rahu will not harm, instead he will create problems and then by your steadfast courage you come out of that with flying colours. From September Saturn went to your eighth house, whatever people say about Ashtama Sani, one thing they agree is that eighth house Saturn guards life, but to get his bliss you need to carry pleasing words(as he sees your second house)carry on work with devotion(he sees your tenth house.

Pisces **Mars**	Aries	Taurus	Gemini **Ketu**
Aquarius **Moon** **Mer**	26thJan 1955: Chennai 18:58 pm		Cancer **Asc** **Jup**
Capricorn **Sun**			Leo
Sagittarius **Rahu**	Scorpio **Ven**	Libra **Sat**	Virgo

This Mercury Rahu runs till June, 2011. The Mercury Jupiter will be definitely better. From October 2013 your Mercury Saturn antara will be far better. The next mahadasa of Ketu(7 years) will make you more and more philosophical and you will have no rebirth.

Generally for Cancer lagna if yogakaraka Mars is in good sthana -9th in your chart - (his compound relationship there is neutral) and when

Ninth house lord Jupiter is in good sthana (lagna -exaltion is perfect) your overall horoscope should be fine. But lagna karaka Moon in eighth house halted many progresses, you are kept in a much lower position you normally would have climbed. Please wear Pearl and feed Crow daily. Date: **10/21/09**

10. MY NEW WIFE'S RELATIONSHIP WITH ALL OF US HAS BECOME STRAINED

Question:

Date of Birth: 05-12-1980
Time of Birth: 14:00
Place of Birth: Chennai
Gender: Male

Thank you for the wonderful work you are doing. My wife and I got married in April 2008. Since then we have been having a lot of compatibility issues. Now, the relationship between her and my parents and even between me and my parents have become strained. My wife and I have attached our horoscope (in Tamil) with this post. We request to you please tell us what is wrong with our relationship, how much will it affect our family, and is it worth for us to carry on long-term. We both are very open to each other and we want to ask for your guidance together. Please be very honest/blunt horoscopically and refrain from providing a marriage counselling. Please let us know our compatibility and predictions for our life together. Just for your record, a lot of the differences between us are related to financial matters, hence; please let us know our financial future together. If possible, please be very specific on dates and months. Our Date of Birth, Time and Place of Birth (for those who can't read Tamil) Boy Date: December 5, 1980. Boy Time: 14:00 HRS Boy place of birth: Chennai (Madras), Tamilnadu Girl Date: February 22, 1983. Girl Time: 18:31 HRS Girl place of birth: Coimbatore, Tamilnadu Thank you so much for all the help and support. Hoping to hear from you soon. Ray and Jan.

Answer:

I can see the problem is only temporary. The Saturn Dasa and Jupiter antara in your chart is the reason for that. Jupiter being the natural benefactor (having 1st and tenth house lordship) having quadrant positioning (seventh house) will normally spoil the place. Seventh house is spouse related. But there is an exception found in your chart that of Saturn is in conjunction with him. The degrees they occupy are 13.3.53 of Virgo for Jupiter and 14.29.22 of Virgo for Saturn. Jupiter in Association with a natural malefic (Saturn in your case) will bound to be neutral to slightly beneficial. Saturn is your eleventh and 12th house lord. Twelfth house is for happiness related to bed and luxurious expenses. Eleventh house is (Labh). Both the planets are in Hastha nakshatra - Hastha is the star for Moon. Moon is your fifth house lord. Fifth house is considered the second best (probably third best if we consider lagna also) to only Ninth house. That is why during Saturn dasa you would have good sailing in most of your life. During this entire Saturn Dasa of 19 years you would have progressed quite a lot. This Saturn Dasa and Jupiter antara Dasa is only for 2 years 6 months and 12 months. During that period you experience all these problems although this dasa bhukthi was the reason for your marriage. The news is this entire

Saturn Dasa will be over on this November 19. (Some calculations may be different in few months or days).

Pisces **Asc**	Aries	Taurus	Gemini
Aquarius	05-12-1980 14.00 hours Chennai 13N05 80E17		Cancer **Rahu**
Capricorn **Ketu**			Leo
Sagittarius **Mars**	Scorpio **Sun** **Mer**	Libra **Moon** **Ven**	Virgo **Jup** **Sat**

Now we see the next dasa of Mercury - Mercury is your fourth and seventh house (again this seventh house - kalathra sthana- is prominent here) lord. As we discussed about benefits having kendra sthana is considered kendrathipathya dosha. But when a kendrathipathya dosha planet sitting in a trine (1, 5, 9) he is considered full subh graha for all purposes. Here mercury is aspected by Saturn and in conjunction with your sixth house (debt enemy sthana) lord Sun. I can say the understanding of each other will be more, all though you will have different view points on most of the things. The same rule applies to your mother sthana (4th house) same mercury having that fourth house lordship. Your father sthana is ninth house and again the dasa planet is in ninth house. I see your ninth house lord Mars being in tenth house helps you quite a lot although he will face harsh realities at the hand of your mother and spouse.

This was from your part. What your wife's horoscope says? Being a Leo Ascendant chart she thinks independently. Her lagna lord Sun is in (again - this seventh house place vital role in your horoscopes) seven. Kumbha rasi is enemic to sun. O.K. what about seventh house lord Saturn, He is in third house- that is good house for Saturn not only that, he is in exaltion there(UCHCHAM). We now consider Klathrathipathi Venus - He is also exaltion in eight houses with Mars (4th and ninth house lord - Poorna Yogathipathi for Leo lagna). Although eighth house is bad many planets, Venus is exception. But I can't say that for Mars. Now the eighth house lord's Dasa (Jupiter) is running, who is aspecting the eighth house, and then

Mars dosha is also reduced drastically. Overall it confirms that there will be some frictions (if you consider difference of opinion as such) but because of her you will get more uplift in life. Her plain talks could be interpreted differently by your parents and vice versa.

I go back to your compatibility test: Naadi Porutham is 8 out of 8. Generally it is considered long married life. Varna porutham is 1 out of 1. The ego problems are mostly absent Vashya porutham is 2/2 meaning mutual attraction and affection. Taara porutham is 1.5/3 that is about health, longevity- that is very fair. Biological compatibility Yoni porutham is 2/4, that is good. Graha Maitri (outlook, objectivity and Intellect Company) is 5 out of 5. Problems I can find are in Gana Porutham - temperamental- 1 out of 6. Bhakoota Porutham - Financial, Socio Economic, Family development issues 0/7. Please digest that it is not necessary that the other partner need be identical. Mercury dasa for you will be financially more stable but can't avoid debts. Build your wealth based on equity from leveraged borrowing. Her Jupiter dasa has no problem affecting your finances.

11. URGENT TIME TO SCHEDULE C-SECTION SURGERY AVOIDING GANDA-MOOLA AND GANDAANTA:

Question:

Date of Birth: 02/02/1974
Time of Birth: 5:10am
Place of Birth: Firozpur
Gender: Male

We are expecting our baby soon; need a c-section surgery within next 7-8 days. My concern is the ganda-moola & gandaanta timings during this period. What times are auspicious for scheduling the surgery? Please specify a range of time for each date as surgery can be delayed a few hours beyond the scheduled time. We are located in Elk Grove CA USA so note our time zone and place.

Answer

Hi, these times don't fall into the category you fear.

19-10-2009 14.10 hrs to 16.50 hrs Elk Grove time Capricorn and Aquarius Lagna 19-10-2009 19-35 to 23-40 Taurus and Gemini Lagna 20-10-2009 the same two times 21-10-2009 4.35 to 9.25

Date: **10/18/09**

12. I AM FORCED TO RESIGN BY MY MANAGER WITHOUT ANY MISTAKE BY ME:

Question:

I AM WORKING in Dubai. I was forced by my manager to submit my resign on 08.10.09 without any mistake or non-performance. I was very frustrated in my current job due to difference of opinions with my colleagues and superiors. I am working for last 8 years with current employer with best performance without any bad remark or loss to my company. (I have sincerely contributed to my company). Now I would like to know: 1. Will management accept my resign or I WILL BE TRANSFERED to another division? 2. Will I get job in Dubai in next 2-3 weeks or I have to go back to India? I am trying very hard and few interviews already given (GOING INDIA NOT EASY DUE TO LOANS COMMITMENTS HERE IN DUBAI.) Details of my wife (if reqd.) DOB: 21.08.1972 POB: PUNE TOB: 16.23PM Details of my daughter (if reqd.) DOB: 12.11.2008 POB: DUBAI TOB: 10.39 AM

Date of Birth: 31-03-1968
Birth Time: 22.32pm
Birth Place: Pune, India
Gender: male

From: -- R....... Dubai
Date: **10/17/09**

Answer: Dear R.., Can I give pointed answer to your question please?

You are running Rahu Saturn dasa/antara - Both are in fifth house from your lagna (Scorpio). Fifth house is the house indicating the relationship with Manager. Before September Saturn was also transiting in your fifth house. That's why lot of rift between you. Now that you submitted your resignation after the transit of Saturn to Sixth house (This is really good period in gochara). Rahu and Jupiter are in your tenth house in transit. Jupiter's position is not good, but when he is with another planet he cannot do any bad to your job prospective.

Pisces **Sun** **Sat** **Rahu**	Aries **Moon** **Mars**	Taurus	Gemini
Aquarius **Mer** **Ven**	31-03-1968 22.32 Pune **18n32, 73e52**		Cancer
Capricorn			Leo **Jup**
Sagittarius	Scorpio **Asc**	Libra	Virgo **Ketu**

Totally you will be better off with this resignation. On your side, don't worry about the manager, as you already submitted resignation; Pick up your phone-talk to his superiors and tell that you are willing to continue if transferred from this manager. Please keep it mind that you don't ever tell anything wrong about him. Superiors don't want to hear that. To keep this option as bird hand.

You will sure be in employment - no worry. You will get another offer in Dubai with better perspectives. This is where you are going to, but when two employers ask you to join, see how elated you will be.

If this happens positively as I mentioned (only if it happened), can you donate to Udavum Karangal, Chennai (Destitute home), whatever you can? If so please leave a note in the thank advisor link. If not also you can leave a note.

Your child is too young to be considered in conjunction with your horoscope.

Your wife runs Rahu - Ketu Dasa/antara -From second and eighth house and in transit also they are in the same place. It is not a coincidence -It is Astrology pointers. Saturn is in 10th house -it has destabilisation effects. I can say the new job initially could be with single status/or you could decide to be there for some time as a single and then bring back your family.

Date: **10/18/09**

13. TOP SCHOOL EDUCATED ROMANTICALLY INVOLVED AND DEPRESSED:

Question:

Date of Birth: 19-01-80
Time of Birth: 10:07 AM
Place of Birth: Vijayawada
Gender: Male

Dear Astrologers, I am a 29 single male. I have been living in US for about 5 years now. I had an excellent education on scholarships from top schools in India and US. I was romantically involved with a girl for 5 years and ended the relationship in Jan 2007. Ever since I have been very unhappy, almost depressed and lost my confidence. I am extremely unhappy with my job too. I know I am capable to do much better in my career but have not been motivated enough. I am very concerned about my career. Even though I earn handsome salary here, I feel very unsettled and as a result I could not choose a girl for marriage so far. My parents have been searching for a girl since 2 years but nothing is working out. I have a lot of interest in going for higher studies (PhD) but I need to marry now. Below is my DOB detail. Could someone please analyse my planetary positions and advice? I wear a silver chain with a silver ganesh pendent. I also have a pearl in Gold ring and will soon be wearing a Coral in

Silver ring. Greatly appreciate your time and help. DOB: 19th Jan 1980 Place: Vijayawada, AP Time: 10:07 AM Please advice on my career. I feel that once my career is on right track I will be ready for marriage immediately. Thanks, Anonymous

From: -- Anonymous United States
Date: **10/13/09**

Answer:

Pisces **Asc**	Aries	Taurus	Gemini
Aquarius **Ven** **Ketu**	19-01-80 10:07 AM Vijayawada **16n31**, **80e37**		Cancer
Capricorn **Sun** **Moon** **Mer**			Leo **Mars** **Jup** **Rahu**
Sagittarius	Scorpio	Libra	Virgo **Sat**

Exactly when your Jupiter Saturn dasa started the break happened. You must have heard that Jupiter is good, etc. But here he is in the 6th house (enemies, breakups) that too in retro and Saturn in 7th house in retro these are the responsible planets. Being the twelfth house lord in seventh (kalathra sthana) Saturn created the break. Being the eleventh house lord he is capable of bringing in another wife (literally it is second wife/love).

Jupiter Mercury dasa is starting on 12/June, 2010. Anyway Jupiter is aspecting second house, twelfth house (the happiness in bed) Mercury being 7th house lord in second love sthana of 11. What else can I point out? A detailed explanation will confuse you. The second love is coming exactly in Jupiter Mercury dasa antara. It could be informal relationship in the beginning, to go along with the retro sixth place positioning of Native lord Jupiter.

Good you Strengthened fifth lord Moon who is in 11th (again get that second love) by White pearl on gold (your native Jupiter) Please take away any silver that is association with 3rd and eighth houses - that is one of the reasons for the break - Coral is fine as the ninth lord Mars aspecting his own ninth house brings you plenty in the form of lotteries and investments from borrowed funds.

Date: **10/14/09**

14. FIXED MARRIAGE BROKE THREE TIMES FOR MY BROTHER:

Question:

Date of Birth: 12-07-78
Time of Birth: 05:10 am
Place of Birth: Bhuj (Kachch), Gujarat
Gender: Male

Respected Group Members, I am asking a very interesting query about my cousin brother & I thing all learned astrologers will help us in this. Actually the query is related to his marriage. His parents started looking for his match 3 years ago. Here the interesting thing is that the marriage got fixed 3 times in these 3 years. 1st time the marriage broke after 15 days of fixing. Second time, Engagement was also done & it broke 5-7 days after engagement. Third time it was height. The marriage broke days before the actual marriage date. Even invitation cards were distributed among the relatives. I want to know what is wrong in his chart. Why his marriage is breaking after gets fixed & finally when will he get married & how will be his married life? The boy is M Tech (Computer Engineering) presently working in America, and a bit headstrong & impatient type of person. His details are: D.O.B: 12/07/1978 TIME: 05:10 AM PLACE: BHUJ (KACHCHH DISTRICT), GURARAT. Best Regards

From: -   Anonymous   India
Date: **10/12/09Answer:**

Pisces **Ketu**	Aries	Taurus	Gemini **Asc** **Sun** **Jup**
Aquarius	12-07-78 05:10 am Bhuj **23n16, 69e40**		Cancer **Mer**
Capricorn			Leo **Ven** **Mars** **Sat**
Sagittarius	Scorpio	Libra	Virgo **Moon** **Rahu**

Hi, you got a kind-heart to help your cousin brother. Best of luck to you.

In his horoscope there is Kalasarpa Yoga= When all planets are hemmed in between the Nodes (North & South Nodes, Rahu & Ketu), Kalasarpa Yoga is formed. This is a very malefic yoga. Rahu spoils suhasthana. Rahu in addition is with Moon the second house lord, creates moody behaviour and harsh vocabulary.

Apart from that in the last three years Saturn was in 12th house. You must have heard about 7 1/2 years of Sade Satte, which is responsible for his problems. From the 12th house Saturn is aspecting 2nd house (family, speech- the impatience is also by that that will also clear now) Now the Saturn has moved to his 1st house, things will settle somewhat.

It is better for him to marry in a sub-Registrar office (non-traditional marriage indicated) and then perform the regular Vedic marriage. Definites are Pooja at Kalahasthi for Rahu Preethi.

As Jupiter the seventh lord is aspecting seventh house, there will sure be a marriage and good married life.

For gems and related aspects to prevent this happen, I welcome direct question through my site.

15. RAHU DASA TO JUPITER DASA, FINANCIAL AND MARITAL BETTER OR WORSE?

Question:

Male - d.o.b 7-4-1984 3.40 a.m. Chennai. I think I am running Jupiter dasa now. Do you think I will be better off in Jupiter dasa than Rahu dasa in financial matters, education and marital matters?

From: -- Anonymous Unknown
Date: **09/30/09**

Answer:

Thanks for the 1-on-1 query. Your lagna is Aquarius, Moon Sign Taurus. Birth Star: Mrigasirsha.

You are right; you have got Jupiter dasa and anthrax now. Prior to this your Rahu Dasa in fourth house and in association with 6th house lord Moon gave you lot of problems in degree education, had problems with your relationship with mother and a spouse also. I think such spousal relationship has broken down now once the Jupiter dasa started.

Rahu dasa for you was showing you all mirages and imaginations, but nothing happened in real. Because of your strong Mars, you might have got chances in Sports field, but your Rahu didn't allow you to gain anything substantial there. Fortunately Mars's overall strength got you some stable jobs to your liking, beating your competitors, hand down in promotions. Because of strong Mars in association with Ketu you would have landed in some Health industry devices manufacturing.

What will happen in Jupiter dasa? Jupiter is in his own 11th house. 11th house is laabh sthana and purposeful travel sthana. It is a sthana for second wife also- I want to forget this nomenclature as there are no 2nd wives allowed by law. But for those people, who faced some difficulties about spouse, separations, divorces, it is a god sent gift.

From 11th house Jupiter is seeing third house (Mars's house strengthened and your career prospects strengthened as well) and thereby your fifth and 8th house lord Mercury. You will develop very good character now; you will be straightforward now that was not there in your Rahu dasa. Another aspect of Jupiter is on your fifth house that of professional or higher education and association with Gurujis, masters, royal people, etc. You will pursue higher studies and will be successful there. Your relationship with Government will be very good now. You will meet Gurujis and Yogis and get their blessings that will guide you through your rest of life. He is aspecting your seventh house that of friendship and spouses, as I said before your marital, spousal relationship gets strengthened. Seventh house lord Sun is in second house with Venus(exalted), I think your spouse will be from Royal or at least very wealthy, famous family.

Jupiter is in mooltrikona in 18.31.17 degrees of Sagittarius

18th degree of Sagittarius is denoting Royalty (Ref: http://www.astrologyweekly.com/dict...) He is in pada of Poorvashada your 4th and 9th house lord. Your prosperity will be related to house/land/

(business-related to finance (because Venus is in second house)/Governmental matters-contracts, etc.

When lagna lord (Saturn) is uchcha in 9th house Libra, we can give 70% to your chart, once again when seeing three planets - Venus, Moon and Saturn in exaltion in very good places (9th house bhadaka for Aquarius lagna but when Saturn is in neecha sthana in navamsa that is nullified- and strengthened) and two planets Jupiter and Moon are Mooltrikona and Jupiter in his own house - what else can any other astrologer say about this horoscope. It is rare to see these kinds of horoscopes. It is not less than Royal.

16. FACING LEGAL CASE FOR GIVING INVESTMENT ADVICE:

Question:

Date of Birth: 09-05-1973
Time of Birth: 4:58 AM
Place of Birth: Chhibramau - Dist. Farrukhabad, Uttar Pradesh
Gender: Male

D.O.B: 9th may 1973 time 4:58 am place: Chhibramau, up, India. One of my clients has complained against me for wrong advising on an investment product which has turned bad. Now this problem is bothering me since November 2008. Earlier on 15 January 2009, client has written a complain letter to local financial regulator in Dubai mentioning the case, prima faci - client has signed all the docs, and my bank supported me. Now client is threatening to file a legal case in financial court, which may affect my career? will it affect my job also in my present bank ... client was travelling now coming back to Dubai on 10 October 09 and after that he may go to court ...this is going on for last one year will there be solution in my favour and when will I be tension free from all this ..

Answer:

Asc: Aries, Ashlesha, Moon sign Cancer.

You are running Venus dasa (2nd and 7th house lord) and Saturn (10 and 11th house lord) Antara dasa. Venus is in your second house along with Saturn. Both of them are aspected by

Neech Jupiter and Mars. Due to Lordship of 11th house from Moon sign Venus is Bhadhakesh. Although Venus puts you in financial advisory, there may be some times when you exaggerate a matter you will be affected. From this time onwards please stick to basic truth.

Pisces	Aries **Asc** **Sun** **Mer**	Taurus **Ven** **Sat**	Gemini **Ketu**
Aquarius **Mars**	09-05-1973 4:58 AM Chhibramau **27n09**, **79e31**		Cancer **Moon**
Capricorn **Jup**			Leo
Sagittarius **Rahu**	Scorpio	Libra	Virgo

In November 2008 you had Sade satti when Saturn was in your second house from rasi. At that time your words/explanations would have created problems.

You know what, now Saturn has moved to your third house. Anybody who opposes you will either be defeated or will come and appreciate you now.

Don't worry too much. Venus and Saturn are incapable of creating havoc in your life, they can give small troubles and with that they are waiting to present you great money and opportunities. Your bank will not let you down, as they will also be affected. They will go and make a compromise rather. They will be covered by professional indemnity, so they are not going to pay him/her, only the insurance company will. Insurance company is not your boss, don't worry then.

Date: **09/30/09**

17. OH... SO MANY HEALTH PROBLEMS!!

Question:

I am going through a very bad phase health wise. My health, which was just okay till last year is now deteriorating. I have heart disease, type 2 diabetes, obesity, sleep apnea, venous insufficiency and back problems. Will I get better, or like my father, pass away early? I don't care for myself, but want to live for my wife since we have no children

Date of Birth: 12-11-61
Birth Time: 11.44 p.m.
Birth Place: Indore
Gender: male
From: Anonymous Petaluma, CA
Date: **09/30/09**

Pisces	Aries	Taurus	Gemini
Aquarius			Cancer **Asc** **Rahu**
Capricorn **Jup** **Sat** **Ketu**			Leo
Sagittarius **Moon**	Scorpio **Mars**	Libra **Sun** **Mer** **Ven**	Virgo

Answer:.

Dear ..., I am sad to hear the health problems. For 12th Nov, 1961 11.44

p.m. Indore, Asc is Cancer, Purva Shadaya nakshatra Sagittarius rasi.

You are running Rahu dasa (running from Asc) Moon (in 6th -health problem-house.) This brought ill-health and probably some phobias and schizophrenic conditions.

When Moon antara dasa goes away and Mars anatara starts, there will be big relief. When Mars antara goes, it is also good bye to Rahu dasa. Then comes Jupiter, although Jupiter is in debilitation, its association with Saturn and Ketu will make it a strong candidate for recovery and rejuvenation.

In transitory chart also, now Saturn has gone to ten from nine, your fears and thinking in terms of father's diseases, will change now., In 2 1/2 years he will move to 11th house, when you will feel like a King and think you got a rebirth not only health-wise, but money wise also.

You have your eighth house lord Saturn in his own house, in a strong position; you will live much longer than your father.

Anti-oxidants in Goji berries, Pomegranate, Green tea are very good cure for your problems.

Date: **09/30/09**

18. LOT OF OBSTACLES AT WORK:

Question:

Date of Birth: 10-041969 Time of Birth: 21:00 Hours Place of Birth: HO – GHANA WEST AFRICA The latitude and longitude of Ho, Ghana is: 6° 36' 0" N / 0° 28' 0" E Makar rashi Ascendant/Lagna - Scorpio Birth star-Sravana, 2nd pada. Gender: male

Greetings Sir/ Madam Is my career is bright? I work very hard and I do have a good position in my current job but facing lots of obstacles lately at work and in closing my deals? Any chance of improvement? When? Last 3 quarters have been really tough. I currently work abroad for a medium sized Indian company I think it's time to move on. When will this happen? I have applied to some good companies have got responses but they have gone cold. Why? Will my next job be with an Indian firm or foreign firm? How high will I rise in my career? Will I achieve top position? When and how will this take place in the coming years? Will I be strong financially? What will be the specific level of financial stability will I achieve. I want to achieve fame as well. Will I do business or continue to work? I know I am under the Jupiter Mahadasa now how do I take advantage? I have been blessed with a wife and 2 kids – but I am not content with my career in spite of working hard and being talented. I do want to scale heights with my career. Please advice and send comments with remedies God Bless

From: Anonymous   Singapore

Date: **09/30/09**

Answer

Dear ..., First of all, when lagna lord Mars is well positioned in his own house in a trine as well as Kendra, your overall horoscope score should be above average.

Pisces	Aries	Taurus	Gemini
Sun **Mer** **Ven** **Rahu**	**Sat**		
Aquarius			Cancer
Capricorn **Moon**			Leo
Sagittarius	Scorpio **Asc** **Mars**	Libra	Virgo **Jup** **Ketu**

Then we consider the most important fifth and ninth houses which should be strong for a strong horoscope. Fifth house lord Jupiter in labh sthana (his enemic positioning cancelled by retro motion) and his aspects fifth house and ninth house lord along with other planets. Ninth house lord Moon gets drishti of Jupiter and (third and fourth house lord) Saturn (deb) considering lagna, fifth and ninth house with other planets, your overall score jumps to 65% where average is just 40%. For your job prospects Tenth house lord Sun in fifth house gets Jupiter drishti and association of exalted Venus and eight and labh house lord mercury, as well as Rahu. All these planets get Jupiter drishti. You can climb up in your profession, as much as you want, but because of eighth house association and Rahu, there will be always some mountains to climb and obstacles to shatter.

From Lagna Saturn now transits in 11th house this is the best period to try for top positions. Again when Saturn transits 11th from Makar Rasi in 5 year time, another jump can be expected. Next job will be with MNC with Indian firm association.

Jupiter mahadasa, for you is second and fifth house lord and natural dhanathipathi in eleventh house (retrograde-nullifying enemic positioning). On the other way he gets aspects of Venus, Mercury, Sun as well as Rahu and connected with Ketu. When Jupiter is conjunct with Ketu in astrology it is called Guru Chandal Yoga. Ketu takes all the good qualities of Jupiter and acts on its own. Therefore my advice is to strengthen Ketu as well as Jupiter by wearing Yellow Sapphire in right index finger. Cat's eye in left middle or ring finger.

Red coral in left index finger. This will bring out the best of this dasa.

Most of your problems were related to 2 1/2 years of 8th house (Ashtama) Sani from Rasi and 10th house Sani(transit) from lagna(hindrance or hard work and obstacles to career progression) Now that he already moved into 9, and 11 respectively most of the clouds will wither   away.
Date: **09/30/09**

19. I DON'T KNOW MY DATE OF BIRTH, STILL, CAN YOU CAST HOROSCOPE?

Question:

I am a postgraduate in Mathematics. I am a male, living in Chennai. At the time of School admission my parents gave wrong birth date and sent me to school when I was preschool age. All that I know is I was born in September, 1968 in Chennai. I don't know the date. I tried with Corporation, but there also record is wrong as I was born in my house. My father said that I was born in the early morning at 5.45. Is there a way to get my horoscope?

From: -- Anonymous Unknown
Date: **09/30/09**

Answer:

Hi ...., it is not as hard as you think. I can exactly give you your horoscope by explaining how I do it. First of all, your father might have given you a name corresponding to your nakshatra at the time of birth-normally. In Chennai more than 90% of people give names on the first one or two letters of babies based on their nakshatra. (What if it was not your case? We will examine it later on)

As your name starts with The/Thea, I go back and search for what this letter stands for. Uttaraphalguni and Rasi should be Leo.

Having understood your Rasi and Nakshatra I go back to Panchank and see on which day this Nakshatra and Rasi falls in September, 1968. On 22-9-1968 5.45 a.m.Moon sign is Leo and Nakshatra is Uttara Phalguni for Latitude/Long 13n05, 80e17.

Now I create full horoscope for you and attach it with this answer.

Pisces **Rahu**	Aries **Sat**	Taurus	Gemini
Aquarius			Cancer
Capricorn			Leo **Moon** **Mars** **Jup**
Sagittarius	Scorpio	Libra **Mer** **Ven**	Virgo **Asc** **Sun** **Ketu**

How to check whether my inference is correct? Now I analyse the horoscope, to see whether there are Planets that indicate your Masterate degree in mathematics.

For mathematical Masterate Mercury, Venus, Jupiter, Mars and fifth and ninth house lords should be in good position. In second house, Venus (second and ninth house lord is in Mooltrikona, in association with friend Mercury. From Moon lagna fifth house lord is Jupiter, he is seeing that house from moon lagna. Jupiter is in friend's house. Mars is in moon lagna in friend's house not bad.

Considering these planetary positions I think your horoscope is correct. You can use this for your future reference. Best   wishes

Date: **09/30/09**

20. DAUGHTER'S RELATIONSHIP WITH BROTHER, SISTER AND MOTHER:

Question:

This is my daughter's particulars. I would like to know how her relationship with brother and sister and mother and father is. What are her career prospects and marriage prospects; once she gets married will it last and also will she get married to someone of same religion?

Date of Birth: 09/06/1989
Birth Time: 8.25a.m
Birth Place: Ascot, England
Gender: female
From: -- .... England
Date: **09/28/09**
Category: **Astrology**

Answer:

Hi, your daughter's lagna is Cancer and Mars is sitting there. Although Mars is in Neech (debilitation). (Your question and concern about her relationship with brothers and sisters in her chart is related to third house, eleventh house and Mars in general) I am seeing whether there is Neech bhanga for Mars. Neecha-Debilitation, Bhanga-Cancellation Raja Yoga- Kingdom

Pisces	Aries	Taurus **Sun** **Mer** **Jup**	Gemini **Ven**
Aquarius **Rahu**			Cancer **Asc** **Mars**
Capricorn			Leo **Moon** **Ketu**
Sagittarius **Sat**	Scorpio	Libra	Virgo

When a Poorna Yoga Karaka is in debilitation, then Neech is cancelled or Neech Bhang happens. In your daughter's horo Mars being the lord of

5th and tenth being poorna yoga karaka, the bhang happened.

Second rule is the lord of the sign of debilitation is in kendra from lagna or moon. Lagna Karaka itself is Moon he is in Leo. Leo being the first of kendra sthana from Moon itself, the Raj Yoga happens.

So her relationship with brother/sister should be with lot of discussions and arguments but it is for totally beneficial and long lasting.

Guru drishti Koti Punya. Jupiter aspecting seventh house and seventh house lord Saturn in sixth in retrograde motion and Venus from laabh from moon and raja yoga karaka (Mars)drishti to seventh house indicates her marriage would be normal, fruitful long lasting. Although Saturn is her seventh house lord from lagna when Jupiter and Mars(neechbhanga raja yoga) sees her seventh house I can say marriage will be to the satisfaction of all concerned, religion/caste may not play a big part in the decision making process. Mars's Raja yoga will get her excellent career as doctor/physio/teacher/nutritionists/realtors.

Father will be in very good term in the long term. Mother will have small quarrels

Date: **09/28/09**

21. IS THERE A LOTTERY YOGA OR LOTTERY DASA PERIOD?

Question:

DO.B. 7-4-1984 time 3.40 a.m. Chennai Can you please see if there is any lottery yoga is there for me and if so when can it happen?

From: -- Anonymous Unknown
Date: **09/28/09**

Answer:

Dear best wishes, your asc is Aquarius. You run Jupiter dasha and Jupiter Antaradasha. Jupiter is the lord of second and eleventh house in your chart; he is running the dasa sitting in Eleventh house (Labh sthana) in Mooltrikona. He is aspected by your lagna karaka (incidentally lagna becomes one of the trines and one of the quadrants. He is in 18.31.17 degrees in Dhanus, in Poorvashada nakshatra (Your full yogakaraka-Venus nakshatra). Your poorna yogakaraka is Venus, he is sitting in Dhana Sthana, do you know how- exhalted and sitting on Saturn's legs in Uttrattadhi. Saturn (exalted) is sitting in Venus's house in nine. Jupiter aspecting fifth house Lord Mercury as well as aspecting Mercury's house Gemini. Lagna aspected by Dairya sthana and karma sthana lord Mars. This is the most benefits planetary position for bountiful wealth with very strong lagna, 2nd house, fifth house, eleventh house, lagna karaka (exalted and sitting in 9th house) ninth house.

For sudden wealth we can see eighth house, which is aspected by Venus of all planets. Eighth house lord in Dairya sthana is aspected by none other than Dhana Karaka Jupiter as well as your lagna lord.

Definite sudden wealth is predicted, that will come in Jupiter Dasa, Jupiter antara, Mercury antara, and mostly in Venus antara. It will happen in Saturn antara also, but Saturn being the twelfth house lord, there will be equal expenditure for pleasure.

When Saturn transits in 3rd house, 5th house, 6th house, 9th house and 11th house (all from Rishaba-your Rashi) you will have big windfalls of money. Same way small fortunes can be expected when Jupiter transits in 2,5,7,9 and 11th houses from your Rashi Rishaba.

When you get windfalls, please try to help Gurujis, Astrologers and destitute children, and then your fortunes will stay with you.

Date: **09/28/09**

22. SATURN MALEFIC OR BENEFIC FOR ME:

Question:

What are the role of nodes in my chart and how they are affecting the chart? Whether Saturn malefic or benefic for me gives the percentage wise means how much percentage he is malefic or vice versa? One astrologer told me to Wear Emerald in Rt Hand Middle and WHITE DIAMOND / WHITE SAPPHIRE to be worn in ring finger. How do you judge? You peoples are wondering that why I came back with my horoscope. See my last query has not been answered by many prominent astrologers among you. DOB:-05th July 1977 Birth time:-20:20pm Birth Place:- Miraj, Maharashtra, India

From: -- .... United Arab Emirates

Date: **09/27/09**

Answer:

Pisces **Ketu**	Aries **Mars**	Taurus **Ven** **Jup**	Gemini **Sun** **Mer**
Aquarius **Moon**			Cancer **Sat**
Capricorn **Asc**			Leo
Sagittarius	Scorpio	Libra	Virgo **Rahu**

Saturn is benefic being your ascendant and second house lord - no confusion about natural malefic nature or badhaka sthana occupancy- Also he is aspecting your lagna from seventh house lagna which is one of the trines (the most benefic places in horoscope)

as well one of the quadrants (the next benefic places) - A malefic having quadrant lordship itself will make it temporal benefic for a native. In your case he is not only having quadrant lordship but also occupying a quadrant, apart from his trine (1, 5, 9) lordship. In Navamsa he is strong in Capricorn. He is in Karkataka 22° 04' 11" Asleesha Pada: 2- (on the pada of ninth house lord mercury) Sama Mitra/Shatru in Kumar /Jagrut Avastha - Parivarthan between moon and Saturn in their houses- It is coming to 72% benefic and the remaining 28% malefic nature comes because of the drishti of Mars and maraka/badhaka sthana relationship of 2nd and 7th houses. If time permits I will try to answer your other separate question about right and left fingers, etc.

Date: **09/23/09**

23. BEST METAL TO FIT BLUE SAPPHIRE FOR ME:

Question:

Which is the best metal to fit Blue Sapphire for me as per my horoscope?In which metal it will give maximum benefits for me best alternative?I don't want general answer.I need specific answer to my query and suitable metal to my horoscope or best alternative only.In his new book Ancient Astroligical Gemstones and Talismans Mr.Richard Shaw Brown II mentions that Solar/Lunar metal to be used: Gold Alternate metal: Iron.So what is I want to wear Blue Sapphire in gold than it will yield full results as wearing it in Iron is not practical.

From: -- .... United Arab Emirates
Date: **09/22/09**

Answer

Silver for strengthening Venus - friend of Saturn- alternatively White gold, as white color neutralizes gold to fit into your scheme of things as per horoscope. On its own Stainless steel is an alternative in isolation for Blue

Sapphire as solar/lunar credentials are met.
Date: **09/23/09**

24. HUSBAND ASKING ME TO LEAVE MY JOB:

Question:

Hi, I am ka.ar. born on 26th november 1980,place valavanur tamilnadu villupuram district time 10.15 am. now i have come for a month to london.my husband is asking me to leave the job and be here for two years.should i leave my job. Please advice and it is urgent.

From:........bangalore
Date:**09/15/09**

Answer:

Rasi Cancer- Asc Capricorn - Mercury Dasa Mars Antara dasa - Mercury being 6th and 9th house lord in 10th house tells that you will have secure/good jobs. His association in 10th house with Venus (Kendrathipathya dosha)makes oscillation in mind about jobs. The recent transit of Saturn to your 3rd house makes sure you will be successful in any ventures now. Ninth house lord is responsible for long term settlement in foreign countries, when he is in Chara rasi(Libra)more likely you are more likely to settle abroad in Anglo Saxan countries.

Pisces	Aries	Taurus	Gemini
Aquarius			Cancer **Moon** **Rahu**
Capricorn **Asc** **Ketu**			Leo
Sagittarius **Mars**	Scorpio **Sun**	Libra **Mer** **Ven**	Virgo **Jup** **Sat**

25. MY SOFTWARE BUSINESS IS ON THE VERGE OF SHUTTING DOWN:

Question:
Date: **09/21/09**

I have started a software business in 2004, however in the last year and a half business has been very bad and the company is on the verge of shutting down. I am also very unhappy with my career choice and feel that my education, natural ability and intelligence are not being justified by my present occupation and work. Will this situation change or will it get worse? Will my financial situation improve or will it get worse?

Date of Birth: 02-03-75
Birth Time: 13:10
Birth Place: Mithapur, Gujrat India
Gender: male
From: -- .... Mumbai, India

Answer: Dear ....., Software business is affected world wide, Market mechanism works against it; you are not exception. People who want to flow with their business plan are shattered to see the entire world change volte face in short time. If you want to revisit the strategy available to you and to your core business pl email with details to erpsolns at gmail dot com, your positions could be seen from out of the square and suggest remedies for a fee.

Pisces **Ven** **Jup**	Aries	Taurus **Ketu**	Gemini **Asc** **Sat**
Aquarius **Sun**			Cancer
Capricorn **Mer** **Mars**			Leo
Sagittarius	Scorpio **Rahu**	Libra **Moon**	Virgo

Gemini Asc: Change and freedom is what they like, but they hardly get. Considering your sade satte and your Saturn Dasa (running from Asc - lordship of 8th(most malefic) and 9th(most benefic) houses) and Rahu Antaradasa (sixth house lordship for Rahu is good, I can say there is no need to be disheartened. Courage (sixth house Rahu) and desire to change will take you through better times.

It is not only necessary to find out what you want in your life, but the key to success is to stick to the path that gives you total satisfaction in long term. Fifth house and twelfth house Lord Venus in 10th house with 10th house lord Jupiter gives you edge in IT- I would say changes within IT sector with flexibility for your time and resources.

26. NUMEROLOGICALLY RIGHT NAME FOR COMPANY:

Question:

My brother-in-law is a very talented, running a company called Tirupathi .in Mumbai. He is going through a bad phase and his last sixteen proposals have been rejected. He wants to know numerologically what would be the right name for his company and also what color should be the logo. Also, are there any Gods he should offer special prayers for. Thanks SK

Date of Birth: 3-Nov-1975
Birth Time: 12.20 a.m.
Birth Place: Mumbai Gender: male
From: Petaluma, CA,USA
Date: **09/19/09**

First of all, about what is going on around the world. When a deep recession and correcting phase struck the world, it is not unusual that new/amended proposals getting rejected. Understand the life principle of the fittest/strongest adapters survive the best. Things are not the same any more, when he understood the changes, he will make big breakthrough. If you want some financial advisor to look at from a neutral angle and give a good advice please ask him to send full details (full confidentiality assured)

Pisces **Jup**	Aries **Ketu**	Taurus	Gemini **Mars**
Aquarius			Cancer **Sat**
Capricorn **Asc**			Leo
Sagittarius	Scorpio	Libra **Sun** **Moon** **Mer** **Rahu**	Virgo **Ven**

Astrologically and numerologically, anything happening in this world will affect individuals to lesser or greater extent based on the strengths of their horoscope, names, numbers.

Your b-i-l runs Saturn Dasa and Venus Antara Dasa. For Capricorn asc Saturn and Venus are good. In his horo they are 7 and 9 respectively in neutral/friendly signs. Seeing horoscope Sure the rejections are only temporary. Seeing the transitions of planets in a normal way, 7 1/2 year Sade Sathe just now started for him from moon sign Libra. But as his lagna is stronger than moon sign, I can calculate Saturn's position from lagna - Capricorn and can conclude that his bad period of Ashtama Sani from Lagna was the reason (for the rejection of 16 proposals - may be in the last 1 to 2 1/2 years) and as Saturn has already moved into 9th house and it is giving breathing space for him to change and prosper. Being native of Capricorn - Saturday and pradosha period Shiva darshan and Navagraha worship will slowly change his fortunes to the better.

There are 11 letters in his name. Those 11 letters total to 47. There are 5 vowels and 6 consonants in his name.

His life path is 9. Destiny path is 2. His Inner or Soul's Urge Number is 6: This is spiritual and emotional expression more than physical. It is his heart-felt desires, his incentive, how he looks at life. Here are his areas of personal satisfaction. Number: 6

His desire, responsibility, steadfast love, a harmonious home, domesticity, and maintaining long-standing family traditions are the perfect environment to have ease, comfort, beauty, music, and harmony.

He empathizes with those who, through no fault of their own, are suffering. He is sympathetic to the needs of humanity. If he knows how, he would correct all injustice as a cosmic parent or guardian would. He has a good sense of loyalty and is a natural counselor.

Artistic, kind, understanding, inclined toward conventionality but broad-minded are other traits. When his emotions aren't too involved, he is a fine judge of character.

To align his company name to his life-path 9: Change to Tirupati Associates

There are 18 letters in this changed name. Those 18 letters total to 72. There are 9 vowels and 9 consonants in this changed name.

This name number is: 9

The characteristics of #9 are: Humanitarian, giving nature,

selflessness, obligations, creative expression.

Also Soul urge number for this will become 8 to align with Saturn. Date: **09/21/09**

27. THREE TIMES MISCARRIAGE:

Question: Gender:female

I am in trouble, not able to conceive, three times major miscarriage in the month of 6+. I had done many remedies, as predicted by many astrologer, but no success, problems with health as well as uterus, periods are not normal or absence, no medicine is suiting, what is the reason when i will be a mother. Regards, kr

dob 20.10.1981 time 19:30 gurgaon From: -- kr India Date: **09/06/09**

Answer:

Pisces	Aries	Taurus **Asc**	Gemini
Aquarius			Cancer **Moon** **Rahu**
Capricorn **Ketu**			Leo **Mars**
Sagittarius	Scorpio **Ven**	Libra **Sun**	Virgo **Mer** **Jup** **Sat**

Taurus Asc Cancer Rasi: You are running Mercury dasa and Saturn antara. Mercury is (28.48.46) in Molatrikona on Chitra (Mars). On its own, Mercury, the fifth lord in fifth should have brought children immediately. The problem I see here is that of Jupiter (28.32.23) in conjunction with Mercury. One concept of Karako Bhava Naasthi applies (Putra Karaka Jupiter in 5th house in enemical position along with Saturn and Putra lord). The other house to see for child for ladies is 9th house. Ketu sitting (in uttarashada) there also creates some problems. But I feel Ketu dasa will make you a mother, as he is aspected by Jupiter. Jupiter's aspect is good for children. Ketu dasa is Starting at 2009-11-16 ~ 02:34. You have come to the astro forum in Ammas at the right time. No need for any parihara. You will have children, be relaxed.

Date: **09/07/09**

28. SCIENTIFIC AURA THERAPY RESULTS SUPPORT YOUR VIEWS ABOUT GEMS FOR ME:

Question:

Chart Already given

Rudra Center in India is world famous for its quality products and now they are doing online aura therapy which will clearly tells us 1) Which is your malefic and benefic planet? 2) Which gemstone or set of stones suit you 3) Which chakra is blocked and how to open it After taking suggestions from you peoples I have checked my aura with Rudra Center which is online now They found that Jupiter,Mercury,Mars,Venus and Saturn are the benefic ones and Sun,Moon,Rahu and Ketu one are malefic. And they suggested me to Wear Blue Sapphire in Rt hand mid finger in Silver and Red Coral in Rt Hand ring finger in Copper. They said that after wearing these two my body aura increased by 300 meters. And when White Sapphire is mixed with combination it reduces body aura and when Blue Sapphire and White Sapphire tried together White Sapphire is decreasing the aura and finally only White Sapphire tried but aura increases not that much. So finally they say the best set for me is Blue Sapphire + Red Coral. What is your suggestion on this? If you will look this combination from astrologically then how they will work and what are their effects? Generally after how many days these Vedic gemstones will give effects? Which is quick result giving Vedic gemstone list them in ascending order with respect to their effects?

From: -- .... United Arab Emirates
Date: **09/03/09**
Category: **Astrology**

Answer:

I have developed great love and affection for you in the short time that you raise these questions, as you strive hard to bring the best in Astrology, which will be good for the entire world. Now that the developed world looks for guidance from the east for many answers to failing financial, health, pension, systems, we dig deep into Astrology too. For universal usage we need to bring it to closer to all other sciences. Astrology is very close to be included as one of the sciences for diagnosing and remedying health problems, employment and marital matching, Planning for good and bad events, etc.

Pisces **Ketu**	Aries **Mars**	Taurus **Ven** **Jup**	Gemini **Sun** **Mer**
Aquarius **Moon**			Cancer **Sat**
Capricorn **Asc**			Leo
Sagittarius	Scorpio	Libra	Virgo **Rahu**

I told in my previous answers that you can wear Blue Sapphire and Red Coral - and many questioned me about the enmity of Saturn and Mars, but point is strengthened by your experimentation. I don't know whether you tried Diamond to strengthen Venus as suggested by me, in the experiment, if you do so, then the aura may increase as well. White sapphire (as your Jupiter is not good for you, being 3rd and 12th house lord), will sure decrease your strength. You need to include diamond in the combination.

Blue sapphire/Neelam shows its effects sooner than any other gem. It is proved fruitful or effective to the wearer, it will destroy his diseases, faults, sorrows, poverty and increases his food grains, prosperity, strength, glory, life-span and off-springs. It also restores the property which the wearer might have lost prior to the wearing of the blue sapphire. If it is proved unfavorable, it may make all the efforts, activities fruitless and may destroy every thing of the wearer.

Blue sapphire is most useful especially to the transporters, property dealers, engineers, contractors, mill owners, dealers in machines, laborers, hawkers, policemen, workers of local self-government and financiers. In Rasis it is good for Capricorn & Aquarius. It is also said that it can give peace to the heart of the man if it is worn near the heart, that is why middle finger(saturn-lordship) near the heart line is considered Saturn finger. Evil thoughts are destroyed and mind as well as behavior remains pacified by wearing blue sapphire. It should be taken off, if its colour is changed or it is cracked. They said wear it in silver to strengthen Venus by that metal.

Third speedy stone Red coral is ruled by Mars. Coral can be worn by those for whom Mars is lord of an auspicious house in the birth chart, of course for you it is!Red coral transmits the cosmic color yellow, which is related to blood, bone marrow, lymph nodes, and the head. Red coral can thus help improve diseases caused by an afflicted or enemical Mars or any relating to the above parts of the body. Red coral also affects the genitals, and works with the immune system, can cure smallpox, fever, headache, jaundice, blood diseases, anemia, weakness, typhoid, allergies, cough, bronchitis, pneumonia, wounds, measles, piles, cough, chickenpox, and problems with bile. Red coral wards of ill effects of debts.

Second place goes to Diamond, which lasts long. Diamonds are the one of the hardest substances on earth. It is next hardest only to the heart of a "Paapi who ill-treats his mother".Wearing diamonds promotes material happiness, life span, prosperity, comfort, good harvests, artistic ability, creativity, marital happiness, physical and mental purity, patience, fearlessness, and good manners. Diamonds also create good feelings in social and family life, help the wearers make proper decisions, help alleviate legal difficulties, build determination, help the wearers to move up in the world and to not waste time. They make wearers successful, ambitious, and able to live a luxuriant life. They bring influence that helps wearers control their enemies for good causes, create feelings of loyalty, pleasantness, and innocence. Wearing diamonds also protects against evil spirits, curses, a snakebite, and Tantric curses. A good diamond can protect wearers from thieves,debts, fire, floods, and poisons. Please see this blue sapphire and diamond combination-this sort of thing will work for you, apart from separate red coral ring: http://www.youtube.com/watch?v=1PG C...

Date: **09/05/09**

29. EFFECTS OF SATURN, JUPITER AND RAHU KETU TRANSIT FOR MY FAMILY:

Question:

Analyse in details about Coming Saturn,jupiter and Rahu&Ketu transit on my and my wife horoscope.Give full /in depth details with manual calculations of each transit and its effects for both of us.I dont want simply software generated details.Consider ashtakavarga,running DASHA/BHUKTI and other relevant details and let us now in percentage wise good and evil results if possible.I will request you to consider either lagna of natal moon or both of them (which ever is most correct as per your view).Let me know any major highlight or major news for me. Check any gain in wealth is indicated for both of us due to transit I am wearing 6ct blue sapphire in rt hand mid finger,whether it will be an advantage or disadvantage during saturn transit?.My wife is wearing emerald,pearl,white sapphire whether it will be an advantage or disadvantage during saturn transit?Additionally she has to wear blue sapphire or not? 1)My Birth Name:-KKR DOB:-05th July 1977 Birth time:-20:20pm Birth Place:-Miraj,Maharashtra,India 2) My wife Name:-BKR DOB:-30th August 1980 Birth time:-16:30pm Birth Place:-Ghataprabha,Karnataka,India (Latitude 16:25:00 North Longitude 74:75:00 East)

From: -- .... India
Date: **08/31/09**

Answer:

Pisces **Ketu**	Aries **Mars**	Taurus **Ven** **Jup**	Gemini **Sun** **Mer**
Aquarius **Moon**			Cancer **Sat**
Capricorn **Asc**			Leo
Sagittarius	Scorpio	Libra	Virgo **Rahu**

With the transit of the Saturn, Jupiter, Rahu and ketu - in the next 2 1/2 years: The coming transit of Saturn from Leo to Virgo will make it 8th house from your Rasi, Aqu. People talk about ashtama Sani as the worst period, etc. But it is not that bad for you, in fact it can bring some fortunes for you. First of all its transit away from 7th will improve your spouse's health and wealth. Your friends will be helpful hereafter. From seventh house Saturn saw your ninth or Bhagyasthana that was your complaint about fortunes not coming through. Now that Saturn has moved, your Bhagya sthana or the fortune sthana is strengthened, now you can expect some big fortunes. So far Saturn was seeing your rasi; you were dull, irritated and lazy. Now when Saturn moved away from 7th you become more active. Saturn was seeing your 4th house, that of house,mother/motherly figures, vehicles, jewellery, dresses,General Sukha,etc. You had problems and difficulties in them so far. Now they change for the good.

Saturn in 8th is not very good for cashflow. But unexpected income may knock your doors; Rather than the expected normal cash flows. Please consult eye doctor if you experience even the slightest of eye problem. Please be careful in your words, there will be more times when you can't keep your words. You will have extended hours and irritation in your job. Your responsibility keeps increasing. Anything that your children do, please keep your cool and talk softly.

Pisces	Aries **Moon**	Taurus	Gemini **Ven**
Aquarius			Cancer **Rahu**
Capricorn **Asc** **Ketu**			Leo **Sun** **Mer** **Jup**
Sagittarius	Scorpio	Libra **Mars**	Virgo **Sat**

For your wife Saturn is moving from the 5th house to 6th. This is best to get rid of your debts. Relationship with husband will be the best. The aspect of Saturn on 8th house will bring unexpected backdoor income.Now expenses through her will be in control as Saturn's drishti of twelfth house is there. She will show courage and help you in dealing with your financial problems. The Saturn in 6th is the best part of 30 year period.

For you, Jupiter transit is not that good in the first year, creating positional disadvantage, but next year in second house he will give you lot of wealth. Rahu's transit to 11 is the best for the planet. All windfall wealth can be coming through. Ketu in 5th house not good for children, please take extra care about them.

For your wife Jupiter going to 11th house is good financially. Try to invest or buy lottorey in her name when Jupiter is in Aquarius. Ketu in third house makes her strong in mind and guies you through. But Rahu in 9th brings problem with her father/father like elder's health.

Date: **09/03/09**

30. LIFE EXPECTANCY, GRANDHCHILDREN AND FOREIGN SETTLEMENT:

Question:

How about health? Will i settle in foreign country or india? How will be my children and grandchildren? What is my life expectancy?

Date of Birth: 09-08-1938
Birth Time: 5:53pm
Birth Place: podagtalapalli near rajahmundry,Andhra pradesh
Gender: female

From:Keywest,,FLORIDA,USA
Date: **09/01/09**

Answer:

Amma, Capricon is your lagna as well as rasi. It is a Chara Rasi. People born in Chara Rasi have more chances (than sthira and upaya rasi) of settling away from their home. Your Saturn dasa is ending in 2011.Saturn being your lagna and second house lord in dairya sthana in retrogade motion in Revathi nakshatra- He made you undertake journeys (3rd house is for short stay journeys) - being on the Revathi(6th and 9th house lord mercury pada) tedious but long stays during Mercury antara and sukshma happened. Now from 2011 you will have Mercury dasa, Mercury's 6th house lordship is nulled by its postiion in 8th and raja yoga in the form of some unexpected financial gains possible. 9th house lord in 8th house indicates, you will have multiple to and fro journeys between India and foreign country- but will have comforts in the stay.

Pisces Sat	Aries Ketu	Taurus	Gemini
Aquarius Jup			Cancer Sun Mars
Capricorn Asc Moon			Leo Mer
Sagittarius	Scorpio	Libra Rahu	Virgo Ven

Your fifth house lord Venus is friend to your lagna lord. Venus in 9th is the best for your children. They will be very very good. No worries at all about them and your grandchildren. Although the Ketu in 5th house makes you philosophical about children, meaning you love every children as your children. This is hard to get an attitude.

About your health as I said before, when Mercury being the lord of 6th house running his dasa from 8th house, your life expectancy gets strengthened, although you will encounter some difficult periods.

2018-2019 Mercury-Sun dasa bhukthi - will be marka like period. If you and your children do Mrithunjaya japam during that period you can overcome this difficult period, then your next bad period is only Mercury Saturn- From April, 2028

Date: **09/03/09**

31. SOME ASTROLOGERS SAY MY SON WILL BE BRAHMACHARI FOR LIFE:

Question:

Date of Birth: 5 april 1990
Time of Birth:12:30 pm
Place of Birth:delhi
Gender:male

Is marriage in my son's destiny? Some say that in his chart, Venus is too far from sun and hence he will be a brahmachari. Please tell if he'll marry.

About the qualities/nature of his spouse and marriage (love or arrange?).Also about the year of marriage; will he marry late or early? When? Will he have a well settled life with children? how many children will he have and of what gender?

From:Anonymous,India
Date: **08/31/09**

Answer:

Dear Sir, It is too early to worry about the marriage.

I analysed his chart. He is born in Cancer lagna and Rasi. Venus dasa is running from eigth house. Someone must have talked about Vedha Avasathai of Venus and Sun in Aquarius and Pisces, where Sun moves a little bit away from Venus. Then Venus will have faster movement and then retrogate. This is common for these rasis. This has no connection with marriage.

Three planets are in 7th house especially exalted Mars. Although he is joined by Saturn and Rahu, please be advised to get him a girl in whose horoscope similar Mangal strength is there in 7 or 8.

He will have love marriage seeing the rahu ketu position. Marriage wile be little bit dragged.Fifth house lord exalted with Saturn and Rahu. I would say he will have Boy and two girls.

Jupiter aspecting Venus makes his wife beautiful.

Pisces **Sun**	Aries **Mer**	Taurus	Gemini **Jup**
Aquarius **Ven**			Cancer **Asc** **Moon** **Ketu**
Capricorn **Mars** **Sat** **Rahu**			Leo
Sagittarius	Scorpio	Libra	Virgo

Date: **09/01/09**

32. SHOULD I RESIGN AND GO TO INDIA TO TAKE CARE OF MY FATHER?

Question:

I was born on 27th June 1979 in Mumbai at 11 am. I am going through a personal crisis because my father is very sick and in India while i am in US. Also, my career is doing very badly. I live away from my husband because we have jobs in different places. I frequently think of resigning since i cant cope up with my job. Please help me decide what decisions i should take- should i resign and join my husband? Should i move to India and help my parents? If not, will i do well in my job?

From: -- ...New Jersey, USA
Date: **08/30/09**

Answer:

Cancer Rasi, Leo lagna - Ketu dasa and Mercury Antaradasa is running for you. There were some difficult planetary positions during Last 7 1/2 years. One of them was Sade Sate - When Saturn is in 12th, 1st and second house from Rasi, these 7 1/2 years will give lot of problems to the native.

The happy news is this long period will be over in few days. Then Saturn in your 3rd house will give you more than what you suffered.

Pisces	Aries	Taurus **Ven** **Mars**	Gemini **Sun**
Aquarius **Ketu**			Cancer **Moon** **Mer** **Jup**
Capricorn			Leo **Asc** **Sat** **Rahu**
Sagittarius	Scorpio	Libra	Virgo

You are having the last phase of ketu dasa in mercury antara. Out of all the planetary periods, that of Ketu is perhaps the most difficult to predict, the reason being it has a tendency to either show the results of the house it is in or the planet it is associated with or the kind of aspect it is receiving and more commonly these three factors show contradictory results. Lack of prudence and mental restlessness was seen in the last 7 years. There was lack of happiness, increase in physical hardships, conflicts with family members and mother obstacles in education and wealth. There could was failure, loss of wealth, harm and trouble caused by the state and by those in positions of authority and a possible fear of theft, poison, water, fire and weapons.

So you understood the two problematic combination of dasa as well as transitory position of Saturn will be over soon.

Your next dasa will be Venus Dasa. This will run for 20 years. Venus is your 3rd (courage) and 10th (job, karma) house lord is placed in 10 in association with Mars, the 4th and 9th house lord - Yoga karaka. That is really good. Although there is kal sarpa yoga (meaning all the planets in your horoscope are hemmed in between Rahu and Ketu) in that yours is Anant Kalsarpa Yoga - Rahu in Lagna, Ketu in seventh house: The person is prone to be target of conspiracies hatched by close people. The person is likely to lose out in matters of courts. Married life would be marred by differences or keeping away one partner from the other.

These problems were exaggarated in Ketu dasa. This will definitely change for the better.

There will be changes to your career. Try something new, different. You will be joining your husband. There will be improvement of your father's health, but it will not be completely different from what he used to have.

You need not move to India. Ninth house (long term foreign settlement) lord is in association with Dasa karaka, you will have very comfortable stay outside. Although Venus has kendrathipathya dosha, his association with Mars (though he is in enemic place) will be beneficial. Your life will change for better.

Date: **09/01/09**

33. WHICH PLANETS ARE RESPONSIBLE FOR MY ANGER, JEALOUS AND ERRATIC PLANNING?:

Question:

Please check which planet is responsible for this 1) I am very short tempered. 2) I am of revengeful nature 3) Highly suspicious 4) Highly jealous

5)Very Very selfish in nature,thinks about my self only. 6) Erratic in planning, never planned anything specially finance hence i am suffering now. 7) Religious, god fearing but whenever try to meditate never succeeded.My mind is always thinking about future.I am unable to control my mind. 8)Expenditures including monthly poojas to deities across leading Indian temples,donations to temples etc. 9)I am fond of self praising,whenever anybody appraise me i am very happy vice versa. Even after these faults I am came up in my life and today whatever position i am standing it is due to my self effort.I am a great devotee of Lord Shiva never live without him.Devotee of Bhagwan Vishnu also. Now tell me after studying my nature which planets are behind this? Saturn is benefic or maraka?What is the role of Mars,Jupiter,Mercury,Sun and Moon? Seen many answers but unable to judge which planet is good one or which is bad one?

From: -- .... India
Date: **08/28/09**

Answer

By constant questions you are encouraging Astrologers to analyse and discuss about finer points of astrology. You are almost making this facility, unknowingly or knowingly, into a Public discussion which will educate many students about our ancient Science.Once again our thanks for that. I keep this question as to explain about just your mind as all the 9 points you raised are concerned about mind and moods (even the 8th point I take it as about the mind to spend on those things). For Mind now we will analyse in simple parlance about lagna,3rd 5th house as well as Moon. Moon is the ruler of mind and moody nature. Lagna is seen for Quality of mind Third house is for the courage/cowardice,chastity (both for ladies and gents),crooked/plain thinking of mind 5th house is concerned with intellect of mind(logical analysing)

First thinking about Moon in your chart- it has got enemical properties to disturb your total mind. The reason moon is taken to represent mind may be about its waning and waxing properties. A person having strong moon will have the mental will power to go in one direction in most aspects of his life (also other planets affect this). Your Mars, Venus are strong enough to take you through in your educational and professional fields. But when it comes to your day to day life the moon's effect will be there that is why moody nature prevails.

Pisces **Ketu**	Aries **Mars**	Taurus **Ven** **Jup**	Gemini **Sun** **Mer**
Aquarius **Moon**			Cancer **Sat**
Capricorn **Asc**			Leo
Sagittarius	Scorpio	Libra	Virgo **Rahu**

Now we discuss about the quality of mind as affected by Lagna. Your Lagna lord Saturn (7th drishti) and Jupiter(9th drishti) are aspecting your lagna. The 9th drishti of Jupiter is considered more powerful than its other drishtis. Lagna lord is aspected by

Mars.I consider Saturn, Mars and Jupiter's karkathvas to decide about quality of your mind. No.1, 2, 3, 4 are by these planets. Also reasons for 5 and 9 are part of Mars aspecting lagna lord.

Second is about the real courage and plain/crooked thinking. Ketu sitting in third house alternates your spiritual thinking.Ketu is Gnana karaka. He is the most powerful of all planets. He makes you to think about religions and charity spending. He doesnt allow you to settle in one of thinking, Oscillation is the mental process given by ketu, to go in depth about any subject. For concentration in meditation you need the strength of Jupiter, it is lacking,.The third house lord in 6th house (in low strength) - brings out any bad karakathvas of the Jupiter. No.5, 9 -Selfishness Self praising are some of them. He initiates his other house (12th)'s job of spending -constrained to his domain of religion and religious expenditures.

Now about the 5th house: Venus gives you some authority on mind over matter.When you talk about No.6 Erratic- I say, your inner consciousness as dictated by Venus and very weak

Jupiter says that everything you can do at the eleventh hour, or you dont need any planning, that's why you managed everything by mental plan rather than real written down plan or discussed plan. This makes you say you are in charge of your life by self-effort.That's real that is your strength. For discussing and structuring your plan your third house should have been stronger. But your fifth house is doing what is good for you without those plans. I answered the questions of good or bad planet in previous answer. Best of luck!

Date: **08/30/09**

34. MOST MALEFICS IN DESCENDING ORDER

Question:

DOB:-05th July 1977 Birth time:-20:20pm Birth Place:-Miraj, Maharashtra, India I believe most malefic planets in my chart are Sun, Moon, Rahu, Ketu and Jupiter (not sure about Jupiter).Whether you peoples agree with me? If yes than let me know which are the most malefic ones (descending) as per combined lagna, Chandra kundali and navamsa chart? Why it is so? How they spoiling my game (life)? What are their aspects and which house they are aspecting and its effects (for each planet give aspects and effects)? By appeasing which planet my wealth increases and how? Check the effects of planets with respect to Nakshtra on which they are placed during my birth? Give me some remedies which are useful in daily life as I am residing in Islamic country and it is not possible for me to perform Pooja of any sacred trees and some other typical remedies. As per my view Saturn and Venus are benefics for me. Mercury not evil even though it is in dustana and Mars is giving mixed results. Are you agreeing with me?

From: -...... United Arab Emirates

Date: **08/26/09**

Answer:

For your lagna Capricon the most benefic is Venus, 1)being the friend of Saturn 2)The lordship of trine(5th) and kendra(10) makes him the most benefic being in 5th, the trine, that too in his own raasi (To show you the contrast of any other horosocope-If Venus was in 4,7,10 kendras for Capricon lagna-then he will have very bad kendrathipathya dosha)3)He is with Jupiter in the trine (He got 3rd and twelfth house lordship- He is in enemical sign -Bad house lordship as well as in enemical position -Jupiter is very weak to disturb the effects of Venus.)4)He is on Krithiga pada - Sun being the 8th house lord - the most malefic lordship- but when I go further and see where Sun is I see he is in 6th house -As the 8th lord is in 6th, the native will experience Vipareetha Raja Yoga results. Affluence and the fulfillment of all desires are some of the resultant results.

Pisces **Ketu**	Aries **Mars**	Taurus **Ven** **Jup**	Gemini **Sun** **Mer**
Aquarius **Moon**			Cancer **Sat**
Capricorn **Asc**			Leo
Sagittarius	Scorpio	Libra	Virgo **Rahu**

No doubt Venus is benefic to you.I would say he is the most benefic to you.

About Saturn: your Lagna and second house lord in 7th house aspecting your lagna cannot be bad. The aspect of his enemy Mars doesnt change that, as Mars from 4th can affect only that sthana not other aspects of Saturn.In Ashlesha (Mercury pada or Sara)6th and ninth house- he is strengthening his benefic results, as ninth house is the most benefic of all trekkanas and sixth house is lesser in significance to that. Lagna is not only Kendra but also one of the trines. Planets having Kendra and Trine lordship sitting in Kendra(it may not be good if it is natural benefic like Jupiter,etc.) having another trine(9th)lord nakshatrapada- I can see he is the next most benefic to you.

That's why in my previous calculation suggested strengthening Venus and Saturn (Diamond and blue sapphire)

Mercury having sixth house lordship and ninth house lordship - as indicated before, the stronger ninth house- lordship should prevail. But one concern is he is in sixth house strengthening debts rather than bhagya.He is on Punarvasu -Jupiter pada -your 3rd and twelfth house Lord. Again he is with Sun your eighth house lord. I would say Mercury's ninth house lordship is very less significant here. He can only do marginal benefits, not much.

A native of Asc (lagna) Capricon wants to wear both, red coral and blue sapphire and Diamond.

The basic principle of wearing gems can be categoriesed broadly into two:

1) To ward of evil of bad planets

2) To enhance the effects of good planets.

Different astrologers have different views about which one is better.

For Capricon Saturn is the lagna lord. Blue Sapphire is considered good to strengthen him. Why would we strengthen him? If he is in good position, by wearing this gem his effects will be strengthened.

What if he is in a bad position? The view is even if he is in bad position he is the lagna lord, everything for the horoscope happens through him.

What if, for the same lagna, the fourth and eleventh house lord Mars is in good position? Here people argue that Mars is enemic to Saturn, but what about fourth house and eleventh house lordship? They may not in fact want, Mars to be strengthless and deter the fourth house and labh sthana karakathva? All the nine planets need be placed in one of the 12 houses in the horoscope. Enmity of planet is only one of the aspects. We need not confuse that here.

Generally speaking, if Mars is strong, courage, land ownership, leadership by strength will be strong in a horoscope. It doesn't matter whether Mars is enemy or friend to a lagna lord. Whatever the relationship of Jupiter for a lagna, if Jupiter is strong, children, higher positions, long term wealth will be good. Here I emphasise, we are not talking about the lordship of houses. We talk purely about the relationship with lagna lord who can be enemic or friend. Red Coral can be worn by the native if Mars is placed in 1, 4, 10, 11th houses. This will ward of his debts. In combination with Sapphire the lagna lord, this will definitely reduce his debt. If you wear Diamond, it strengthens the most benefic Venus to give you more.Here we need not confuse the enmity anymore.

When Lagna is strong, why should consider Chandra Kundali. Navamsa already considered in the form of Nakshatra padas.

When Rahu is in ninth, you will get different meaning of wealth and prosperity.Please understand wealth is a relative term. I give you the Sukshma of getting wealth for Saturn natives. For capricon natives as their lord is Saturn, if you create a cause related to help needy, poor, disadvantaged people, wealth pours in. Create a good cause to satisfy Saturn, when he gives, you can't even count it.
Date: **08/29/09**

35. WHAT TO EXPECT IN SANI DASA,GURU BHUKTHI FOR ME?

Question:

I have recently entered Sani Dasa, Guru Bhukti and would like to know what I can expect during this period and how to best take advantage from it. Also, what areas of my life should I focus my energies on at this time? AlsoI understand that both planets have mixed aspects in my birth chart which will influence this period as well, so any help with that is much appreciated. Born Nov. 23, 1973, 11:32am (2:32am GMT), 129'43"E 33'10"N (Japan), Capricorn Ascendant Thank you!

From: KK United States
Date: **08/21/09**

Answer:

Pisces	Aries **Mars**	Taurus	Gemini **Sat** **Ketu**
Aquarius			Cancer
Capricorn **Asc** **Jup**			Leo
Sagittarius **Ven** **Rahu**	Scorpio **Sun**	Libra **Moon** **Mer**	Virgo

The last period of Sani you have Guru Bhukti. Sani is your lagna and second house lord. Normally lagna and dhana lord sitting in sixth house creates enemies and ailments. But for Saturn (the natural malefic- this rule is slightly different). Sixth house being one of the upajaya sthanas, Saturn in sixth is neutral. When he is combined with Ketu it turns a little favourable. Sani is in Gemini 10-2-47 degrees in Ardra Nakshatra. Rahu is ruling Ardra. Rahu is in Moola- on Ketu pada. Seeing the strength of Ketu who is in the last degrees of Mrigasrsha, during Saturn dasa based on the strength of Saturn, Mars, Ketu you would have good period, in education and would have some financial gains, throughout the period.

Now for the Jupiter Bukthi., he is malefic for Makar Rasi, having third and twelfth lordship. Malefic sitting in lagna is not good. But even though he is malefic for the lagna, his aspects of 5th, 7th and ninth house remain very good. Your higher education or gnana, friends, spouse, father, bhagya, all will be good during this period. Normally Jupiter, will not give benefit to the place he is sitting in being the most benefic generically, wants to help others by his drishti. But as he is a malefic here and he is debilitation, this rule is changed for you. He brings some individuality to your character while others could stamp it as self-centric, dont worry too much about them. In degree 13.28.56 he is on Sravana (lord Moon).Moon is in 10th house. You can strengthen your positions and focus during this period. Concentrate on drawing up your career furtherance plans and the next dasa Mercury being the lord of ninth (sixth house lordship is just some obstacles but ninth house lordship will shatter anything on the path) will take you to victory on your plans

Date: **08/24/09**

36. WHICH FINGER FOR MY RED CORAL RING

Question:

DOB:-05th July 1977 Birth time:-20:20pm Birth Place:-Miraj, Maharashtra, India I have removed my Emerald (given green cloth/pulses in donations on Wednesday) and brought one 3.90ct premium quality White Sapphire and wears in my Right hand little finger (as no space in right hand mid finger due to Large Blue Sapphire ring).How is this combination of Best Premium quality Blue Sapphire 6.22ct in Silver in Right Hand middle finger and Best Premium quality White

Sapphire 3.90ct in Silver in Right Hand little finger? Now I want to wear RED CORAL.Let me know whether it will be suitable wih Neelam and white sapphire or not? If yes, then how should I arrange them to get maximum effects in no time? I want to wear all 3 of them and don't want to miss any gem.So find me thw best way which will bring me abundance/wealth.My only concern is to get rid of my debt and increse my wealth dramatically. Note:-Please members addressing all my above concerns only answer.Dont send me wrong information as last time when I posted my query some members mentioned that my 5th house is Vrishik and Council members had given highest rating to him. Why Council members are blindly giving ratings? From:India
Date:**08/22/09**

Answer:

Pisces **Ketu**	Aries **Mars**	Taurus **Ven** **Jup**	Gemini **Sun** **Mer**
Aquarius **Moon**			Cancer **Sat**
Capricorn **Asc**			Leo
Sagittarius	Scorpio	Libra	Virgo **Rahu**

My honest understanding is that you are going to the extreme about gemstone wearing and astrology as a means of changing fortune. Anything extreme is affecting one's psyche and makes them think about their life from that aspect only. Why can't for a change you talk about real financial problems to financial advisors and draw up an exit strategy for your debt problems and stick with that for some time. Before that, please have your expenditures in excel sheet and discuss with your wife and together you find the heads of exp. that you could cut to make the total of all exp.(everything included) within 75-80% of income.Once did, see how happy you would be. But this is only one aspect. Thinking from lateral point from another relaxing view, when the entire financial systems in the world are faltering and recession is forced on the world, why do you think, you alone are affected by debt problem. There are millions affected as well, with all their life's savings eroded.Think about India debt ridden for hundred years now. You will now feel your problem is not as big as you imagined.

Now about your question as asked, your removal of emerald makes your mind more steadier now, thats right. Sapphire is considered a stone of creative expression, intuition and meditation. It also is said to increase mental clarity and alleviate depression. The gemstone is also said to promote light, pure emotions, such as serenity, joy and peace. Sapphire is associated with the brow chakra.Such as the real Blue Sapphire in middle finger(representing brow chakra) is good.

Jupiter is your courage house and Viraya house lord and having bought White Sapphire and want to wear that, I would say it is better in ring finger.

Strengthening Mars, the debt lord and softening the mercury tendency to borrow, it is better on little finger. I don't find problem in wearing the three of them.

Date: **08/22/09**

37. IS THIS BLUE SAPPHAIREENOUGH?

Question:

I am looking for better job opportunity, currently I am working as a manager with IT MNC. I am wearing Blue sapphaire. Let me know if need to wear any other gemstone to enhance career prospects and when will i get another job.

Date of Birth: 12-03-1973
Birth Time: 21:00
Birth Place: Delhi
Gender: Male
From: -- xyx India
Date: **08/20/09**

Answer:

Asc Libra Gemini Rasi Ardra Star-Saturn Dasa and Mercury Antyaradasa: Saturn is the most benefic for you being the lord of fourth and fifth house and as a friend of your lagna lord Venus. Only problem with him is, he is in eigth house- which is the most problematic house in anybody's chart.But he aspects dhana sthana. In your ninth house, tenth house lord Moon sits with Ketu.Ketu is in debilitation and Moon is more than 11 degrees away from him. I believe the lagna lord Venus, most benefic and best friend of lagna lord Saturn should be strengthened.As, your tenth house lord Moon and ninth house lord Mercury (the 12th house lordship when the planet is in 6th is viparitha yoga, when sixth house lord jupiter occupies a kendra-it is raja yoga as well.) are already strong, no need to strengthen them.

Pisces **Mer**	Aries	Taurus **Sat**	Gemini **Moon** **Ketu**
Aquarius **Sun** **Ven**			Cancer
Capricorn **Jup**			Leo
Sagittarius **Mars** **Rahu**	Scorpio	Libra **Asc**	Virgo

Please wear One ring having Diamond clusters (multiples of 8 - to ward of Venus's eight house lordship) and a sapphire(a little bit violet- not dark blue-to ward of 8th house positioning. It should be on gold, yellow or white. I know it is difficult to find one like that. But the blue sapphire you wear is sort of general remedy it doesn't fit into in depth requirement. Once you wear the recommended ring you can remove this ring and give it to your family. If you have problem finding one please SMS me.

I don't see any reason why it can't happen now in Saturn and mercury Dasa, and when Saturn is in benefic 3rd house in Transition chart. Try very hard in the next few weeks and months.

Date: **08/20/09**

38. PROBLEM OF JUPITER AND MERCURY:

Question:

From the above data, my Jupiter is in the 6th house and its current dasa is running till 2019. Mercury in this dasa is upto august 2010. Mercury is in the 12th house. Could you please tell me how these two planets are affecting my life due to their bad placements? 2. Also I am not going through a good phase as I finished my MBA in may 2009, and currently not doing anything. My parents are forcing me to take up a job but I want to setup some business. Could you please tell what I will be doing? Also maybe what business is good for me? 3. My dad and I are not having a good relationship and we keep getting into fights. What remedy can you suggest and will the situation ever improve with him? 4. My mother happens to be a psychiatric patient. Will she be ok in the future, without any major problems? 5. I have an addiction to cigarettes. Will I be able to stop smoking ever or is this going to continue? 7. I also feel that my manhood maybe be in trouble as I feel I might be going impotent. This may be due to rahu in 1st house? I am feeling shy to ask this but will this situation improve by looking at my chart? 8. When will I get married? Will my marriage be ok or will there be some problems? How will my wife be? Will I have children? 9. I feel really spiritual at times and I have collected lots of books on spirituality. I also plan to setup a ashram sort of place where people can come and meditate, and have lots of other thoughts also about spirituality. What does my chart say about this? 10. I want to learn astrology, is this indicating in my chart? Will I be able to learn it properly and make good predictions? 11. I sometimes feel my willpower is weak, is this indicated in my chart? How can I improve? 12. I want to setup a center for doing research in astrology, palmistry, pranic healing, past life regression, numerology, etc? Will I be doing this in the future? 13. At times I feel like leaving my family and joining some ashram in the Himalayas and doing tapas for the rest of my life? Are these thoughts normal for me? 14. How much money will I make, looking at my chart? Sometimes I feel I understand business so well that I could make lots of money. Is this indicated in the chart? 15. I want to build orphanages and take some active interest in social service, will I be taking up social service according to my chart? 16. Sometimes I feel that to serve the society, I must join politics, I have a keen interest in keeping my self up to date with the latest happenings and I feel I could serve well as a politician for the public. What are your suggestions? 17. I also have a court case pending against me, it was registered in January 22, 2004. Will it be resolved favorable? 18. What are main drawbacks? 19. How can I improve my life? I know I have asked many questions, but I asked whatever came to my mind regarding myself. I would appreciate feedback to help to improve my life. Thank you for your help. Xxxxx

Date of Birth: May 6 1983
Birth Time: 08:33 AM
Birth Place: Hyderabad, India
Gender: male
From: -- ...... Hyderabad
Date: **08/19/09**

Answer:

Pisces	Aries **Sun** **Mars**	Taurus **Mer**	Gemini **Asc** **Ven** **Rahu**
Aquarius **Moon**			Cancer
Capricorn			Leo
Sagittarius **Ketu**	Scorpio **Jup**	Libra **Sat**	Virgo

1, 2 & 4) Jupiter has Kendrathipathya dosha (being the lord of kendras-7 and 10) therefore his placement in Sixth is neutral, not bad at all. He is in the pada of Anuradha(Saturn lordship, Saturn being the lord of eight and nine- you see the problems of eighth house and there are some better things also happening to you now of that of bhagyasthana. Getting an MBA is those of the things associated with Jupiter and Mercury. Mercury being the lord of first and four again, should avoid kendras,that he did- his position in 12th is also neutral because 12th is bhoga sthana. It creates mental worries about mother and makes you think too much and sleepless. I think your mother's problem will be solved next year. For business I see your 4th house lord, as well as Business karaka Mercury- again he is in 12. Business is not so good for you. For job your 10th house lord Jupiter in 6th for me is good, because he is aspecting your tenth house. When Jupiter sees his own house that too 10th house, what elese should I tell. Your job will be very good. He is in Bhagyathipathi as well as Ashtamathipathi Sara. Getting a job is difficult, but once you are on to a job you will progress well. What else, you will be a business Manager, based on the strength of Mars and Jupiter. Take my words for granted you will have a very satisfying career. 3) Saturn being 8th and ninth house lord gives problems with dad. To avoid you can worship Lord Dakshinamoorthy on Thursdays. 5) Saturn in 5th house keeps you out of control and this Smoking is one of the habits people want to avoid. Seeing Mano Lord Sun sitting with Mars, I would say once this Mercury Bhukthi goes, you will try to put an end to it. 7) Again it is not because of Rahu, it is because of Saturn (Manas sthana) and ketu (seventh) who make you think about problems of manhood. If Rahu is in 3rd house, what you fear may be possible, but not for you. Again when Ketu antara dasa finishes after mercury, this kind of feeling will pass off. 8) In Jupiter, Venus dasa, Marriage will happen. Your wife will be beautiful and bold. You will have two (even a twin) children. 9) Ketu makes you think about all kind of spiritual and Jupiter in sixth house helps him. But it will be shortlived, this will change in 2012. 10) For good astrologer, Jupiter, Mercury and Ketu need to be strong. I don't think you have those planets strong enough. But having said that, you can learn astrology, but there will be some limitations. 11&12 &13 &15)For will power see the third house, Sun in with mercury in Uchcha Sthana, you have will power. You can establish bigger establishments, destitute homes as a social service but you dont need to practice mystic sciences.Mediation is good for any age 14) Your money lord Moon is in Bhagyasthana. Bhagya sthana lord Saturn is aspecting second house. Eleventh house lord is good, Twelfth house is good thereby your expenditures will be limited. Ninth house lord in 5th: I feel you will never have big problem with money. You will amass wealth; some lucky winnings are indicated by 8th house lord's fifth house position. 16)You will be good at politics seeing your mars and Sun, and Saturn 17)The court case will be trivial, dont worry too much about it, even if it went against you, there will not be big harm to you 18)Too much thinking, no action. Start doing whatever you think appropriate immediately, thereby avoiding the effects of mercury and giving credence to mars and Sun. 19)You need a five year plan for your life - finances, job, education, marriage,etc. you decide, what you want and write it down on a paper, it will happen to you because of your Mars and Sun. Date: **08/20/09**

39. EXPENDITURE RUNNING OUT OF HAND:

Question:

DOB:-05th July 1977 Birth time:-20:30pm Birth Place:_Miraj,Maharashtra,India (Latitude 16:51:00 North Longitude 74:42:00 East) I am a Civil Engineer working for an American MNC at Dubai,UAE and residing in Sharajsh,UAE with wife ,daughter Of 4 years and a son of 5 months. Wearing a blue sapphire 6.2ct in rt hand mid finger and an emerald of 4.25ct in rt hand little finger. I am wearing a Javanese Rudraksh Indra Mala from last 12 days. Please check my chart for impacts of various planets, dosha, remedies and for any wealth combinations.My expenditures are out of control and debt is increasing day by day.Please find me an effective quick way to move out of this.Check what are the impcts of Saturn transit in September to Kanya on my horoscope.And let me know appearance of which animal in early morning dream will bring abundance/wealth/prosperity.

Date: **08/12/09** **Answer:**

You have Saturn Dasha running from seventh house. Your lagna lord Saturn is dhana sthana lord as well. That means this Saturn dasa will give you transitory- why I tell you, Moon in whose place Cancer, Saturn sits is in Saturn's another house - that of dhana sthana. Moon brings money when in transition it is good. One more thing I saw was Mars aspecting your lagna lord Saturn. Mars is called debt lord. His aspect makes you spend and borrow. I want you to strengthen your Poorvapunya (5th house and tenth house) lord Venus with diamond for you and your wife.

Pisces **Ketu**	Aries **Mars**	Taurus **Ven** **Jup**	Gemini **Sun** **Mer**
Aquarius **Moon**			Cancer **Sat**
Capricorn **Asc**			Leo
Sagittarius	Scorpio	Libra	Virgo **Rahu**

]The Saturn transit normally (from 7th to 8th)is Ashtama Sani. Very bad. But as your Rasi is Kumbh Rasi lord Saturn has 12th house lordship as well. I would say it will not be that bad for you. 12th house lord in 8th house may some time bring lottery or backhand money. You need to have Diamond on you to strengthen your very good planet and Saturn. These diamond ring videos impressed me: http://www.youtube.com/watch?v=_12g...
http://www.youtube.com/watch?v=1PGC...
Date: **08/13/09**

40. SPIRITUAL PROGRESSION AND CHRONIC DEPRESSION:

Question:

Question:

Date of Birth: 20 april 1986
Time of Birth:16:25
Place of Birth:delhi
Gender:female

I ask, Mr R.S, to reply. as per astakvarga,am i a lucky individual? Will i be well off in life? Which are the best and worst areas as per my chart? Suffering from chronic depression and mostly worried.is there any such combination which suggests that? Does chart promise spiritual progression? How spiritual? Kindly give sufficient rationale behind your analysis. From: --
Anonymous India
Date: **08/12/09**

Dear, Please stop thinking that you are alone in this world. You got billions of brothers, sisters, mothers and relatives to help you. Go out of your boundaries to see the world with bright light.

Pisces **Mer**	Aries **Sun** **Ven** **Rahu**	Taurus	Gemini
Aquarius **Jup**			Cancer
Capricorn			Leo **Moon**
Sagittarius **Mars**	Scorpio **Sat**	Libra **Ketu**	Virgo **Asc**

The good news is your stars are changing. In Transition you have Saturn in your rasi and Jupiter and Rahu in enemic sixth house. This is changing soon. Sade Satti-When Saturn is placed in your Rasi (it happens every 30 years)it aspects your dhairaya sthana,friends and spouse sthana and tenth or work sthana. In the last 2 1/2 years everything became dull, not moving forward, laziness crept in, friends deserted, courage departed. Now in September Saturn will go to your second house. Although it is not very good, it is better than the previous 5 years (including when he was in 12th house-Viraya). Things will improve in health, depression will go away, friends will come back, It will create hard work but long term finances will be planned for in this time. Pass this 2 1/2 years planning everything properly, then the next 5 years are going to be your best period.

O.K. now the chart: for your Virgo lagna when looking at your Dasa , Sun the 12th house lord is running it from 8th house, Antara Dasa lord Jupiter - your 4th and 7th house lord(Kendrathipathya dosha) is running it from 6th house. That is why you are mentally disturbed for unreal things.

Spirituality can come from Jupiter, Saturn (5th and 6th house) or Ketu, each one will be different in its manifestation. In your chart as all these planets are not well placed, you imagine spirituality is something about suffering. It is not. Spirituality is about living happily and making others enjoy their life too. Please chant "SOHAM BRAHMA SOHAM VISHNU SOHAM MAHESWARA" meaning Brahma, Vishnu, Easwara,

You and I are one". You are nothing but the Bliss and Godliness of the combination of them.

For overall strength of the individual I look at your lagna lord, Mercury. He is in Pisces 9:53:49 in Uttrattathi-Saturn Star, aspected by 3rd and eight house lord Mars. Your ninth house lord is in 8 with Sun and Rahu - But he is about 22 degrees away from them. Normally 8th house is bad. But for Venus it is not. I would give a value of 60% to your chart.

Date: **08/13/09**

41. SEVERE MENTAL ILLNESS FOR NEARLY 10 YEARS:

Question:

I need your urgent reply, since i have been suffering from a severe mental illness for nearly 10 years now, which could be either depersonalization, or derealization, or both. It may have started earlier, before the age of 14-15, but i felt no such effects on my mind (probably due to my young age). To my mind, these mental troubles are due to lord Rahu, since the mahadasha of Rahu is running now. In fact, i have the impression that lord Rahu is 'occupying my mind' (like in Hindu mythology, Rahu swallowed the Moon). It is a real nightmare! I am really unable to describe my feelings, but in some forums, there are some people suffering from similar troubles, and giving a perfect description of what they feel. Here are my birth details, so that you could thoroughly analyze the matter: - date of birth: 17/03/1986; - place of birth: nearby Paris (49°03'06' N, 2°06'O6'E); - time of birth: 11.25 (in the morning). Please give me some answers regarding the issue. Once again, i repeat that I NEED YOUR URGENT REPLY, even a brief description, no matter. Thanks in advance.

From: SSS,France
Date: **08/11/09**

Answer:

Rahu runs his dasa from eleventh house. He sees fifth ketu that makes you think lot about people. He is in Aswini Nakshatra (Ketu star). The Mano (Mind) karaka and exalted Moon is in the twelfth house (bed time sthana) lordship and aspected by Saturn (eight and Ninth lord), and mano karaka makes you to think about other people who are in trouble. Ketu (Moksha karaka) is in Swathi nakshatra (Rahu nakshatra) although he is in panchama sthana aspected by Jupiter.

Now you understood it is deeply rahu which is giving lot of confusions and the fact that you are able to understand them away from yourself is an indication that it is not realy mental illness. Ketu is trying to open up your wisdom. Some of the so called illusions could be real in earlier lifes, etc. So don't worry about whatever is happening in your mind. Have a strict schedule of your work, it need not be paid. It could be voluntary community work, like teaching children, helping aged people, etc. Engage yourself physically for major part of the day. Your lagna lord Mercury will give you all the bounties in association with exalted Venus. The only way to wade of the effects of moon and rahu is to do your job with devotion, that is enough, don't think too much.

Pisces **Sun** **Mer** **Ven**	Aries **Rahu**	Taurus **Moon**	Gemini **Asc**
Aquarius **Jup**			Cancer
Capricorn			Leo
Sagittarius **Mars**	Scorpio **Sat**	Libra **Ketu**	Virgo

Check your digestive system, eat lot of vegetables, curd, If you can find a Goji juice please take two spoons every morning and night.Avoid fatty, spicy food.

I am sure you are not afflicted mentally; Your nervous system is weak. Lot of physical work, exercises, games, sports will cure it.

Date: **08/12/09**

42. CHARTERED ACCOUNTANT BUT HARDLY ANY MONEY LEFT FOR SAVINGS:

Question:

I am a practicing Chartered Accountant in Mumbai by my profession and I earn good enough but there is hardly any money left for my savings. Hence, will I be able to accumulate wealth in future. 2) As per my knowledge my 7th House of Life partner is not so strong but at the same time I have never faced any such problem with my life partner till now from last six years after marriage and we live very happily, is there any care to be taken in future. My wife date of birth is 11-11-1979 at Ahmedabad-Gujarat-India at 10.15 am. 3) Will I be able to buy my own house in future, if yes, then when. 4) I have heard that I have

Hamsa Yoga & Laxmi Yoga, shrapit Dosha, is it correct, if yes, then what their effect is. 5) Do I have Gaj Kesari Yoga, Neechbanga Goya or any Raj Yoga, if yes, then what are there effects? 6) Do I have daridra yoga and Karl Sarpa Dosha, if yes, then, what are their effect. 7) Please provide a brief prediction on my chart House wise.

Date of Birth: 30-03-1979
Birth Time: 02.15 pm
Birth Place: Pindwara-rajasthan-India
Gender: male

From Kay, India
Date: **08/08/09**

Answer:

For strength of a chart first I see lagna and lagna lord. Your lagna lord is Moon. He is very well positioned at ten. This is excellent for your entire life. Jupiter is a benefic to you being the lord of ninth (the most powerful house in any chart). When he is sitting in lagna your overall horoscope gets strengthened further. But he has another house lordship, that of 6th-Enemies and debt sthana.

That's why your finances are spent on expenses.

Pisces Sun Mer Mars	Aries Moon	Taurus	Gemini
Aquarius Ven Ketu			Cancer Asc Jup
Capricorn			Leo Sat Rahu
Sagittarius	Scorpio	Libra	Virgo

Jupiter in your lagna aspecting 7th house is more than good for your spouse house. I can see Jupiter strengthened your higher education and your position by his aspects of 5th and 9th. Probably an astrologer would have indicated about Saturn and Rahu sitting in house 2(that is general family and dhana house).

Seventh house lord Saturn sitting in house two is not good for retaining money and for general family.

In Your wife's horoscope her lagna lord is sitting in tenth with fifth and twelfth house lord mars and Rahu. Her husband house 7th house lord Mercury (when benefics have Kendra lordship- Kendrathipathya Dosha is formed) should not be placed in Kendras or good places. He is sitting in twenfth house; it is very beneficial to you. Your money is spent on enjoying life, going places, etc, because of your wife. Otherwise it would have been wasted. So your wife's horo is not bad for you.

I have taken all your yogas into consideration and say your general wealth is really good. But you are 1) spending too much 2) afraid of taking mortgages,etc and calculating interest rates,and waiting for rate drops. But from seeing 4th house for both of you, if you determine to have a house you can get it within a year. Later on you will sell that house and get another one. Keep going, enjoy life with own house.

Date: **08/09/09**

43. SISTER-IN-LAW WANTS ILLEGAL RELATIONSHIP:

Question:

Date of Birth: 24-06-1975
Time of Birth: 03:17 PM
Place of Birth:Eluru, Andhra Prdesh, India
Gender:male

Hi, My friend Birth Details: 24 June 1975, Time: 3;17 PM, POB: Eluru, Andhra Pradesh, India. Question: Wifes: 30 Oct 1978, 5:28AM, Eluru. Younger sister: 02 Nov 1980 9:21PM, Eluru. He is married but having frequent turmoil with his wife's sister as both were very much interested before, but unfortunately that marriage didn't take place but instead in a competitive way the boys parents' liked the elder girl only.

The younger also got married with aother boy.

My friend wants to avoid his wife's sister totally from their family. But still the younger girl wants to continue relationship with the friend's family and there is a frequent disturbance in their family matter, is there any affliction to 5th and 7th house in boy's horoscope. The boy is some times under depression and unable to concentrate on his carrier and struggling. When this will end? Any remedy recommended for any grahas. Otherwise, how is his carrier?.

From:India
Date: **08/07/09**

Answer:

Pisces	Aries	Taurus	Gemini
Jup	**Mars**	**Mer** **Ketu**	**Sun** **Sat**
Aquarius			Cancer **Ven**
Capricorn			Leo
Sagittarius **Moon**	Scorpio **Rahu**	Libra **Asc**	Virgo

He got Kuja Dosha, now Mars (kuja) Dasa running from the 7th. Mercury Antaradasa Mercury in 8th with Ketu: What can you expect in Kuja Dasa and Mercury running from the most malefic of houses 8th? Rahu too from 2nd house creates problem in the family. His wife is having Mars in 2nd but with mercury, therefore mostly Kuja dosha is nullified.Jupiter Dasa and Saturn Antaradasa. The problem is about not seeing the Kuja dosha at the time of marriage and then problem with Rahu, Ketu.

Her sister is also having 2nd house Rahu, which makes the case strong for Rahu Ketu Preeti.

For Rahu preethi, do rahukal durgai pujai and for kethu preethi- do Abhishekam for Ganapathy, Do Pradhosha kala pujai in Siva temple.

Date: **08/09/09**

44. WHEN WILL SUN SHINE ON THEIR LIVES?:

Question:

This query is posted on behalf of my friend, who has been suffering for the last twenty years; will they ever see "SUNSHINE" in their life? My friend's DOB – 23.02.1966, Star – Revathi Day-WED, Time- 21.23, POB- Chennai Husband's DOB – 10.07.1964, Star – Poosam Day-FRI, Time- 16.52, POB- Karaikudi Wife's – Sukra Maha dasa since Nov 1989 – Nov 2009 Husband's – Sukra Maha Dasa since Sep 2001 – Sep 2021 now Rahu bhukthi since Nov 2008 also having last phase of Sade Saathi (7 ½ years Saturn) Both are under the influence of SUKRA(VENUS) MAHA DASA, some say that is b'coz of that they are suffering as both life partners should not have the same DASA. 1) Is it so? Both are highly qualified my friend was a govt employee circumstances made her resign and go abroad, abroad though earnings were good it was all spent for her ailing brother. Both are god fearing and believe that Shirdi saibaba is with them otherwise there will no where is this world. 2) No proper job since last ten years for both, will situation improve after wife's sukra dasa is over or 3) Twice business was started in the last decade, but were cheated by people around and was not successful. Now can they start business after completion of wife's SUKRA dasa and husband's saade sathi is over, if yes will someone by god's grace back them financially to commence. 4) Will they ever shine in their life is my final question as both are really frustrated that everything seems very flourishing but when things reaches ripen stage it just withers away be it job prospects, business prospects all these years. Kindly be transparent whatever be and stick to the same horoscope, b'coz things are happening as per this only. Thanks in advance.

OM SAIRAM

From: -- ...India

Date: **08/04/09**

Answer:

SAIRAM for their welfare!! First of all over reliance on astrology and horoscope is not advised. Even if a chart is not good, there are hundreds of quotes saying you can change it by mere perseverance and hard work.

Pisces **Moon**	Aries	Taurus **Jup** **Rahu**	Gemini
Aquarius **Sun** **Mer** **Mars** **Sat**	WIFE		Cancer
Capricorn **Ven**			Leo
Sagittarius	Scorpio **Ketu**	Libra	Virgo **Asc**

Pisces	Aries **Jup**	Taurus **Ven** **Mars**	Gemini **Sun** **Rahu**
Aquarius **Sat**	HUSBAND		Cancer **Moon** **Mer**
Capricorn			Leo
Sagittarius **Asc** **Ketu**	Scorpio	Libra	Virgo

- Normally the logic behind same dasa having problems for couple is if the dasa is bad they will be bad for both. It is only a generic theory. I dont place much importance to it.

- For husband I can say his Rahu Ketu take precedence over other planets. Venus with Debt lord Mars makes the Venus dasa in 6th house problematic.

- Wife's star I am getting is Uttara Bhadrapada and not Revathi

- For wife normally Venus dasa (lord of 2nd (though some consider maraka) and ninth house lord) in fifth house should have done well.

- I see the reason is in doing business and too in foreign country Fourth house is for business successes. Her fourth house lord Jupiter is in ninth- that is very good, but its association with Rahu does the trick. Guru with Rahu is Guru Chandala Yoga. The ninth is the house for foriegn settlement. Jupiter, the badhakesh for this lagna is in association with Rahu (normal malefic as well as karaka for foreign settlement) decieves the benefit that would have been given otherwise.Again four strong planets in the sixth house give

Sanyasa Yoga, where the mind thinks everything is maya, and everything as enemic. The courage sthana 3rd is occupied by Gnanakaraka Ketu.

- Forget about Venus dasa -The next dasa Sun - The other three planets Mercury, Mars and Saturn are conjunct within few degrees but they are not combust. Sun is 11.12.24 degrees in Aquarius. Sun is 12th house lord and his positioning in 6th house gives viparitha yoga- Whether it is viparitha raja yoga is debatable. Sun dasa should be better. She needs to concentrate her business/job region to east. Ask her to place importance to courage and success rather than on mere Vedanta. Most of the time her convictions should guide their future and not her husband's. Clear cut goals and planning, not relying heavily on others advice is what is required in Sun Dasa.

Date: **08/04/09**

45. FOURTH AND FINAL ATTEMPT IN CLINICAL EXAMS:

Question:

I am doing an MBBS (medical doctor) degree, yet it is taking me so long to complete it. I am having so many difficulties; even when I work hard things go wrong. I have just completed my clinical exam,for the fourth time. This was my fourth and final attempt which I had to appeal for after failing the third time.It was so difficult and I can think of plenty of things I did wrong.Others who were doing it for the first time found it easy and it was so disheartening and crushing to realise that despite spending seven years and so much money on the course my mind still went blank, I still did things wrong, and didnt know some of the answers. There are so many people who have helped me, people who are rooting for me and have spent time and energy supporting me. To disappoint them and have them feel pity for me is heartbreaking. I have given all of myself, my time, and energy to this and if I fail they will kick me out. I have spent seven years of my life doing this MBBS degree which I should have finished in five years, and if I fail these exams which I had from July 28-July 31 2009 I will be leaving with nothing to show for it. I will have no degree, and no job prospects. I am 26 years old, and I am gravely worried about this, as most girls my age graduated ages ago, have jobs and are now settling down and getting married. At school I used to be the brightest in the class, had so much promise, but slowly my star has stopped shining, I have gone downhill and everyone is overtaking me. If I fail and get kicked out, and at the the age of 26 am not even a graduate, then who will even marry me? I am very stressed, please can you advise me about my career and financial prospects. Will I ever have a good education and career, and be able to earn a good wage? When will this difficult period end and things become more stable for me? Will I ever get married? I just want to know if there are any chances of good things happening in my life. Will I ever get any happiness? My results for this exam will come out on the 28th August. I am so demoralised, I just want to feel happy again, I want to be able to achieve things, not have my progress in life hindered by setbacks. Thank you so much. By the way, my horoscope is as follows. Lagna is leo, saturn is retrograde, in libra in the 3rd house, Jupiter-scorpio, 4th house,ketu-sagitarrious, 5th house, mercury-aquarious, 7th house, sun, mars, moon-peices, 8th house, venus-aries, 9th house, Rahu-gemini, 11th house. Please be honest and frank with your answers, even if you have bad news, tell me. At least then I know what to expect. Thank you for all your help.

Date of Birth: 15-03-1983
Birth Time: 16:32
Birth Place: Birmingham, UK
Gender: female
From: -- xy UK
Date: **07/31/09**

Answer:

Pisces **Sun** **Moon** **Mars**	Aries **Ven**	Taurus	Gemini **Rahu**
Aquarius **Mer**			Cancer
Capricorn			Leo **Asc**
Sagittarius **Ketu**	Scorpio **Jup**	Libra **Sat**	Virgo

I am really sorry for whatever happened to you. I pray all Gods to help you come through successfully at least this time.

Wishes apart, I checked the reason for the problem, Ketu in the 5th house, aspected by Saturn is not good for higher education. Ketu being Maruthuva planet strengthens it further. Normally Ketu will give all the problems in the first half of his dasa and at the second of his Dasa will turn beneficial. (Ketu Dasa for you started in Decemeber, 2006 - it is 7 year dasa - so I think you are nearly half way through, things should start to look bright from next June. I am not sure about this exam. But there will be a way out for you to get through to medical profession.

I looked at planetary position on the date of your exams. 31st seems to be most beneficial. The other dates were ordinary.

4th house indicates degree level education. Jupiter being the lord of 5th house in 4th is good. But his lordship of another house 8 is what makes you undergo such difficulties. Mars, who is your 4th and ninth house lord is with lagna lord and Viraya lord- The three are in the most difficult place that of 8. 12th house lord Moon in 8th is viparitha yoga. That's beneficial. Lagna karaka in 8th house is itself bad. But when aspected by Jupiter,its ill effects are almost nil. The most beneficial planet for Leo lagna is Mars, his placement in 8th bothered me. But still he is aspected by Jupiter. Jupiter's aspect removes most of the doshas. Venus, the 10th house lord in 9th house makes sure you will have a wonderful career. Jupiter's aspect of 10th house asserts that. Venus in Ketu nakshatra - I would say you will be in gynaceology, natural medicines, non-regular or non-conventional systems.

I dont find any problems with your marriage. Mercury and Saturn are good. Jupiter's aspect of 8th house will remove any Kuja Dosha and Venus is good in ninth. Fourth house Jupiter also good for suha.

Higher education is a late starter but once you get through degree, specialisation will be a breeze.

Why do you want to compare others with you. Who said everyone should complete a degree before 26? I know hundreds who did afterwards and are happy about that as well. Live your own life, which is unique for everybody. One gets certain things; the other gets some other thing. Your marriage life will be very good, that may not be good for somebody else. You career will run like a flow. It will have obstacles for somebody else. Lagna Karaka Sun and your best planet Mars aspecting your second house and second and labh house lord Mercury in seventh is good for net wealth and bank balance in the long run, Jupiter and Venus affirms that. So you are unique, Keep it up.

Date: 08/03/09

46. IAS OR PhD TELL ME:

Question:

Date of Birth: 20 april 1986
Time of Birth: 16:25
Place of Birth: delhi
Gender: female

I am contemplating to give IAS a shot,but on second thoughts,would like to pursue P.hD and go into teaching.Does my chart support teaching and my high career ambitions with any specific combinations? Do i have a government job in my destiny? Of a high strature or a mediocre one?will i ever be able to teach at univ level or remain at school level? Do you see me going abroad specifically for study purpose? If yes, when? Will i settle there? Please elaborate on nature of my career and finances. Again i request ..., Mr. R.S .... to reply.

From: -- Anonymous India
Date: **07/24/09**

Answer:

Virgo Asc., Moon Sign Leo: Fifth and sixth house lord Saturn in its good third house. For good Government jobs like IAS, IPS Sun, Jupiter and Mars should be very good. In your case Sun in Aries is Uchcha. 12th house lord in 8th is Viparitha Yoga. When he is with Bhagyathipathi Venus, I would say it is Viparitha Raja Yoga. Mars has the eight house lordship which is not good but his position in fourth compensates for that. For teaching or IAS/IPS you need strong vocabulary. Ketu in 2nd house aspected by Jupiter gives that strength. Again second house is aspected by Sun and Venus. The kind of authority in words, you have.

Pisces **Mer**	Aries **Sun** **Ven** **Rahu**	Taurus	Gemini
Aquarius **Jup**			Cancer
Capricorn			Leo **Moon**
Sagittarius **Mars**	Scorpio **Sat**	Libra **Ketu**	Virgo **Asc**

Tenth house aspected by Jupiter as well as mars is good for Job. Tenth house lord Mercury in 7th is not good, but considering it is in debilitation, it strengthens your chances.

You can give it a go for IPS or IAS in that order, Viparitha Raja Yoga may help you. Second choice is PH.D.

Foreign study is remote. But you will visit foreign for other purposes. When Jupiter sees your second house and second house lord Venus itself sees his own house, I would say overall finances are very good.

Date: **07/24/09**

47. WANT TO BE HEART SURGEON, IS IT IN MY CHART?

Question:

Date of Birth: April 2, 1987 Time of Birth: 11:08:00 pm Time Zone: 5:30:00 (East of GMT) Place of Birth: 74 E 53' 00", 21 N 21' 00" Shirpur, India Gender: MALE I am living in USA with family, moved here permanently at age 15.I want to become a Doctor (M.D, and later a Heart Surgeon. 1).Is this career line favorable for me?. 2).Will I have success in it, wealth and prosperity wise? 2A). I am currently not in Medical college but going to apply within july(09)- December(09) period ?, will i get admission ? 3).one of the astrologers had told me to do Keelak pooja, should i get it done? 4).How will be my married life? what will my wife look like ?, from where will she be ?. 5). I know hard work is required for real success, but at times i feel lack of motivation or laziness, are there any suitable remedies for me or gemstones i can wear for that ?. 6).ARe there good yogas in my chart?

Thank   you.

From: -- SV v USA
Date: **07/24/09**
Category: **Astrology**

Answer:

Pisces **Sun** **Jup** **Rahu**	Aries	Taurus **Moon** **Mars**	Gemini
Aquarius **Mer** **Ven**			Cancer
Capricorn			Leo
Sagittarius	Scorpio **Asc** **Sat**	Libra	Virgo **Ketu**

Ketu is related to medicine. It is in 11th from Asc, aspected by Jupiter. Ninth house lord Moon is Uchcha and is with Surgery planet Mars in seven. Tenth house lord Sun is with fifth house lord in fifth house. Fifth house is for higher education - and education related to heart and he is with Jupiter). You will be a Heart surgeon, go ahead. Chart is surely favourable for you, but there are lot of difficulties ahead because of Saturn in lagna. Persevere and you will get a good career as doctor. Right now you get 77.78% for transitory positions. Good time now through to October for application.

Wealth and prosperity are relative terms. You will have no problem in normal finances.

Your laziness is because of Saturn's transitory position in your fourth house and aspecting your moon sign. This will change by the end of October.

Chandar Mangal Yoga is indicating a good financial position. The native takes care of a number of friends & relatives. On the marriage front, Mars in 7th house is taken care of by Bhagyakaraka and exalted Moon. Venus position in fourth is good with eighth house lord (Longevity of husband's life). You are young and once after career is settled, then we can discuss about that.

Pearl is what will strengthen your labh planet in bhagyasthana. I dont want you to strengthen Venus or Mercury in Kendra, nor Saturn who is lagna as well.

Date: **07/24/09**

48. 3 YEARS 5 JOBS AND FATHER PARALYSED:

Question:

Dob-17/12/1980 time-01.05: am place-thana (near mumbai) sir from last 4 months i am not on job i lost my job in recession; I have gone through 10-12 interview but got negative result. From last 3 yrs i am suffering from financial crisis as in 3 yrs i have changed 4-5 jobs due to some reason i am unable to attain stability in job, my father also got paralysis at that time and he is retired from service from 3 yrs. Sir i am doining lot of mantra/puja but i do not think any thing is working .every time my work which i think will be 100% done or i will get profit but it do not happen and i suffer loss . So pls help do i have pitra dosh/kalla sarpa or any thing pls guide and do my father also have pitra dosh his DOB is 11/09/1953,time-11.15 pm and place –deg (dist.bhartpur) rajasthan. Pls suggest any remedy for me i am totaly upset. I am doining fast on Saturday and Sunday. I am lighting deepak near peapl tree on Saturday, jaal to surya every day, jaap of shani every day and also mhamurtinjay mantra. Pls help guidance needed of yours thanks,

From.......... India
Date: **07/24/09**

Answer:

Pisces **Moon**	Aries	Taurus	Gemini
Aquarius			Cancer **Rahu**
Capricorn **Ketu**			Leo
Sagittarius **Sun** **Mars**	Scorpio **Mer** **Ven**	Libra	Virgo **Asc** **Jup** **Sat**

When things happen they do in sequence. When you are afraid of one thing, it definitely comes through.I can see two good planets in your dhairya sthana. A bad planet in upajaya sthana will make one strong mentally. A good planet makes the native fickle in mind.In your case two good planets are there. You run the dasha of Venus who is in 3. Please keep confidence in you. It is not in Mantras alone. For dhairya read Hanuman stories. In between search of jobs, do something on you own. There are webbased businesses that you can take up immediately today. If you need any webbased result oriented jobs that you can do in addition to regular jobs, please leave your email, I will send you a list.

Date: **07/24/09**

49. 10 YEARS MARRIAGE, NO PROGRESS 8 JOB CHANGES:

Question:

My husband and I quarrel and fight continuously (sometimes it gets violent). For the past 10 years since we have been married, he has changed more than 8 jobs. He always wants to quit his job. At his current job he only joined 3 months ago, and wants to quit already. He does not want to strive to achieve anything in life. We have so much debt and no savings. I was born as an orphan, so I do not have correct birthdate for myself to tell you to see our compatibility in marriage. We have been married for 10 years and i see no positive signs of our lives getting any better. My question is when will we start to see some fortune/money/real estate in life? My husband was born on June 26th, 1972. His nakshatra is Moola and rashi is Danusu. I don't know what pada he is in. Please help me to understand the life path i am on. Thank you so much for your kind help.

From: -- jji nj, USA

Date: **07/20/09**

Category: **Astrology**

Answer:

As you have not given the time and place of birth for your husband, I calculate only Rasi and Nakshatra and leave out Asc. All calculations are from moon. 10th house lord Mercury is in 8th house (ashtama sthan) along with Mars and ketu. This tells his inclination for job will be least. Through prasna I get current dasha as Moon and Mercury antaradasha.Moon and Jupiter are in Dhanush. Bhagyathipathi Sun is in seventh house. That is why, just because of you, he is able to manage so far. One good thing I notice is that the dhana sthanathipathi Saturn is well positioned in 6th house with sixth house and eleventh house lord Venus. I advice him, to stick with highly paid but odd jobs - any manual jobs involving physical work (lawn mowing, lifting,etc.) is very good and it will bring you prosperity. White collared jobs are not suitable for him. If he sticks with that you will get a house in 3 years time.

Date: **07/22/09**

50. MY EXPENSES ARE MORE THAN INCOME, WHEN WILL I BE DEBT FREE:

Question:

Date of Birth: 09-05-73
Time of Birth: 4:58 am
Place of Birth: chhibramau
Gender: male

When i could be debt free and see strong income flow. My expenses are more than income and it put pressure in terms of credit card debt or personal loan. When can I see real increase in my financial status? When i would be able to purchase house and good bank balance .Am I unlucky in terms of financial stability

From: -- Unknown
Date: **07/20/09**

Answer:

If do.b is Sept.5, 1973 Venus Dasha and Ketu antara dasha for Leo Ascendant Scorpio moon sign, Jyeshta star. Venus neech in 2nd house and ketu in 11th house with 6th house lord Saturn- The financial problem is related to Venus. You need to do Sukra Shanthi.

Pisces	Aries **Asc** **Sun** **Mer**	Taurus **Ven** **Sat**	Gemini **Ketu**
Aquarius **Mars**			Cancer **Moon**
Capricorn **Jup**			Leo
Sagittarius **Rahu**	Scorpio	Libra	Virgo

If DOB is 9th May, 1973 Asc Aries Star Ashlesha Moon Sign Cancer. Venus in 2nd in association with Saturn aspected by mars, jupiter- Lot of confusion about finances in this Venus Dasha and Saturn Antara dasha. 2nd sthana is money and lot many palnets are associated with it in your horoscope. In Transit also Saturn in 2nd house creates cash crunch situations. Overall I would say this problem is temporary and your long term finances are good. Second - your expenses in the medium term-will be over income - to overcome this please say 15% of income you put in savings as an expense now.

Overall Venus dasha should be good for finances, you will buy a beautiful house based on the strength of your 4th house and moon and eleventh house mars. In 1 1/2 years from now, you will see real changes, at that time the Saturn will also be in strong position in 3rd house. Starting from 1-11-2009 you have 3 1/2 years best period for finances and house.

Date: **07/22/09**

51. MARRIED IN 2006 NO CHILDREN, ANY DOSHA??

Question:

My date of birth is 16-08-1973, Time of birth 4.44 A.M, Place of birth: Bhadravati, my wife date of birth is 25-10-1983, time of birth 23.55, place of birth: shimoga, my marriage date is 01-06-2006, When will we have children?, boy or girl ? Do we have any dosha? Is there any puja need to be performed? Pl.help

From: -- somesh mv India

Date: **07/21/09**

Category: **Astrology**

Answer:

Pisces	Aries **Mars**	Taurus	Gemini **Sat** **Ketu**
Aquarius **Moon**			Cancer **Asc** **Sun** **Mer**
Capricorn **Jup**			Leo
Sagittarius **Rahu**	Scorpio	Libra	Virgo **Ven**

Moon sign Aquarius Asc Cancer Star Purva Bhadra Pada Mercury dasha and Ketu Antara

- For cancer - Mars is the full yoga karaka, being the lord of 5th and 10th house. He is in 10th house -that is his own house -is the best for Cancer raising natives.On the sheer weight of Mars (5th and 10th house-

Karaka) I would say there is child it will be male.

- Jupiter the Puthra Karaka is in debilitation in seventh - although I dont rule out Neech Bhang because of the position -that is not good, that is delaying child brith.

- Your wife Taurus, Cancer, Mrigasirsha Jupiter dasha and Antara. Now I understand the problem. Jupiter is Puttra- Karaka. He is in 5th - Putra sthana. The saying is "Karaka Bhava Naasthi". He is stopping the child birth. Association of malefic with Jupiter nullifies or cancells its ill effects. But Ketu with Jupiter is Guru Chandal yoga. Only one thing that tries to solve the problem is 5th house lord Mars from 2nd house sees his own house and aspects both Jupiter and Ketu. Previous dasha was Rahu - aspecting fifth house delayed the marriage.

- Certainly you need Guru Preethi. I saw Guru Preethi Homam can be ordered online. One of the sites I saw http://www.saranam.com/pujas/ho mam_...

- There will be child in or after Guru-Sani dasha-antara.

Date: **07/21/09**

52. WILL MYCHILDREN TAKE CARE OF mE IN OLDAGE?

Question:

Date of Birth: 13 nov 1961
Time of Birth: 5:45 PM
Place of Birth: pahwara,punjab
Gender:female

Correct birth data of my children not available.can you please tell if my children will look after me in my old age? Can you predict anything about my children from d-7?
From: -- Anonymous India

Answer:

Moonsign Capricon, Asc.Taurus, Star uttara Shadaya

Pisces	Aries	Taurus **Asc**	Gemini
Aquarius			Cancer **Rahu**
Capricorn **Moon** **Jup** **Sat** **Ketu**			Leo
Sagittarius	Scorpio **Mars**	Libra **Sun** **Mer** **Ven**	Virgo

- Each child has different houses and characters.It would have been better with their dob. I try to answer in general about children.

- From your querry as you are running Jupiter dasa being the lord of 8th house I can understand there is some concerns on children. Venus being and in 6th house with 5th house lord mercury- its trouble from children Saturn currently inashtama sthana in transit is also not good. Overall this is not a good period. But once you pass Venus Bhukthi and Sun Bhukthi, things would be bright.Also when Saturn goes away from eighth house, things would settle.

- When Saturn, your ninth house karaka is in 9th house, with Jupiter and moon, I think overall your children will be kind and good to you. The one thing I fear is about Ketu, therefore lot of Vignesh Jaba is required. I will hear from you in later years, "Hi my children are the best".

Date: **07/21/09**

53. IS MARRIAGE IN MY CHART, HOW MANY CHILDREN?

Question:

Date of Birth: 5 apr 1990
Time of Birth: 12:30 pm
Place of Birth:delhi
Gender:male

Is marriage in my destiny?or will i never marry? Please tell about the qualities/nature of the spouse and marriage.also about the year of marriage.will i marry late or early? When? Will i have children? How many children will i have and of what gender?

Date: **07/21/09**

Answer:

Pisces **Sun**	Aries **Mer**	Taurus	Gemini **Jup**
Aquarius **Ven**			Cancer **Asc** **Moon** **Ketu**
Capricorn **Mars** **Sat** **Rahu**			Leo
Sagittarius	Scorpio	Libra	Virgo

Moon Sign cancer Asc. Also Cancer: Ashlesha.Venus dasha:

- The question is significant because 7th house is occupied by Mars, Saturn and Rahu, all natural malefics and it is the place for the spouse. The seventh house lord occupying his own house (spouse house) is considered somewhat favourable. Mars is Poorna Yogakaraka for Cancer as such he cannot create problem, but look at how he is, he is exalted. Any Mangal dosha, when he is with containing planets like Rahu and Saturn will be almost gone and it turns favourable. Considering the other lordship of Saturn being 8th, longevity of wife's life is indicated. I would say there will be only minimum problems in marriage. There will be happy married life. Venus Dasa and Rahu Antara dasa is running. Venus in eighth house is not considered bad. But you will have acquaintances with high calibre girls, but you need to be choosy. There won't be any delay in having children after the marriage. Both genders, For Fifth house lord one son, for Saturn association with fifth house lord in own house considering his eighth house adhipathya, thre will be a girl and for Rahu's association there could be one abortion or twins. This will happen respectively when there bhukthi or antara is running.

Date: **07/21/09**

54. DISPOSE FLAT, US JOB OR LOCAL JOB WHICH CHOICE FOR FINANCIAL MESS:

Question:

Date of Birth: 30-04-1976
Time of Birth: 03:02 am
Place of Birth: Bhimavaram
Gender: male

I am having the following options for me to come out of the financial mess i am in. 1) Disposing the flat, which i had taken in jan 2007(i will have to book loss on a/c of this, but i will have peace of mind). 2) Changing the job to get higher income. 3) Trying for a US oppurtunity in the current company. Right now i am exploring the 3rd option.Do you see any success for me in trying for abroad oppurtunity. What will be the best option for me you think i have to concentrate more? one of the above option has to be executed by the end of dec'09 beyond which i will not have any resources to manage. i am very much nervous/tensed and not able to concentrate on anything. to give you an insight on my earlier travels, i travelled/stayed in US may 07 - aug 08. i travellled to other countries between 2002-2007 on short trips spannning couple of months. Please let me know your opinion. my details:

dob: 30-04-1976 tob: 03:02 am place: bhimavaram,A.P wife dob: 10-04-1987 tob: 6.30 am place: palakollu,a.p

From: -- Anonymous India

Date: **07/17/09**

Answer:

Pisces	Aries **Sun** **Moon** **Ven** **Jup** **Ketu**	Taurus **Mer**	Gemini **Mars**
Aquarius **Asc**			Cancer **Sat**
Capricorn			Leo
Sagittarius	Scorpio	Libra **Rahu**	Virgo

In transitory position you score 7/9, that means this is the right time for settling financial matters. Rahu Dasa and Rahu Antara Dasa - Rahu in 9th house-(9th house is Foreign travel and settlement).

I have problem with Rahu being a cheating planet sitting in Ninth house. But when I look at Rahu aspected by so many benefics like Jupiter (dhana karaka , 2nd house and 11th-profit house lord as well)Venus(4th and 9th house lord-very benefic). Rahu is in Visaka Nakshatra the 2nd and 11th house lord.

I am 100% sure you will get foreign job.In the meanwhile even if you sell the flat; you are definitely getting a new house later on. Don't worry. I have never said definitely to anybody else like that. In your case it is real.

55. MY GIRL'S PARENTS LOOKING FOR MATCH, I CANT PROPOSE AS I DON'T HAVE JOB:

Question:

Date of Birth: 29-12-81
Time of Birth:6:30 am
Place of Birth:rohtak
Gender:male

Hi i am.... , i am having an issue with my love life , my details are as follows : full name ...., dob 29/12/1981 , tob 6:30 am(between 6:25 and 6:30

am) pob rohtak haryana , place of residence r.... haryana. I am in love with a girl named k.. DOB 29 Sep 1983 her tob is 10:10 pm (not sure though) place of birth rohtak haryana. now we'r having trouble as her parents are looking for a match for her and I cannot take the proposal to them as I am not working (looking for a job) , Can I know what can I do to help our case as we are desprate to be togather. waiting for reply rgds

From: -- ..India

Date: **07/18/09**

Category: **Astrology**

Answer

Pisces	Aries	Taurus	Gemini **Rahu**
Aquarius			Cancer
Capricorn **Moon** **Ven**			Leo
Sagittarius **Asc** **Sun** **Mer** **Ketu**	Scorpio	Libra **Jup**	Virgo **Mars** **Sat**

Moon Sign Capricon Asc. Sagitarius Birth Star Shravana

Rahu Dasa and Venus Antara Dasa, Rahu in 7th house (house for married life)is not good for proper marriage, Lagna having Sun, mercury and Ketu all aspecting 7th house is not a good indication, either. In transitory positions also you run ashtama sani.

- Your lover moon sign Gemini. Asc Taurus. Star Ardra. Jupiter dasa and mars Antara dasa. Jupiter and Ketu in 7th house and Rahu in Lagna and 9th house lord Saturn(for father's acceptance)in 6th house indicates it is going to be Kantharva marriage without Parental acceptance.

- I checked for the compatibility also. You get 23 out of possible 36- Medium compatibility. But the major aspects are good.

- Away from Astrology I will say you both need to have courage to ask your parents, after all they are the reason for both of your happiness, and if there is any problem in getting acceptance then you should stand firm. Please check with your lover if she can stand the questions of parents or can live without them, before deciding. At least arrange for a temporary job for both of you.

56. WHAT KIND OF MARRIAGE AND SPOUSE, GIVE ME THE RATIONALE:

Question:

Date of Birth: 20 april 1986
Time of Birth:16:25 pm
Place of Birth:delhi
Gender:female

Please give rationale backing your predictions also. please tell if marriage seen in the birth chart? are there any signs of estrangement/divorce/remarriage since venus is in krittika? What kind of marriage and spouse does it point to(profession,characterstics)? What is the possible year/timing of marriage? Does it indicate children? How many and of what gender? Kindly augur on the marriage and progeny, please. Regards

From: -- Anonymous India
Date: **07/17/09**

Answer:

1) House 8 Venus is in 28.35.23 - Kritika - Neutral house 8 Sun is in 6.24.24 - Aswini - Friendly 8 Rahu is in 6.21.43 - Aswini.

- I dont think there is problem with Venus in 8th house.Generally lord of 2nd (family) and 9th house in 8th is bad. But specifically for Venus eight houses is good. In the star of 12th house Karaka also is not a problem. My problem is about Mercury with full Kendrathipathya dosha (good planets with quadrant lordship) in Seventh house. When I saw mercury in debilitation half of the malefic effect is wiped. But in the opposite way Jupiter having 4th and seventh lordship to be in 6th house is good for mrriage life.If Jupiter is in any of the quadrants I would rule out marriage. Mars aspecting 4th house is another bad sign.Second house with Ketu is bad for family life, but aspect of Jupiter and Bhagyathipathi Venus nullifies it. Sun in 8th house is in exhaltion, I consider it like mangalik dosha for mars in 4th house. Overall I would say there will be marriage but there are problems with married life.

Pisces Mer	Aries Sun Ven Rahu	Taurus	Gemini
Aquarius Jup			Cancer
Capricorn			Leo Moon
Sagittarius Mars	Scorpio Sat	Libra Ketu	Virgo Asc

- 1) There wil be marriage. Alternating Hot and cold moods in relationship. 2) Karaka Venus's second and ninth lordship and association with Sun and Rahu and in the house of mars indicates, husband will be affluent, authoritative, and beautiful and he will be a Surgeon. 3) Fifth house lord Saturn in good position (3rd is good for Saturn) and aspecting his own house says there will be girl child. Jupiter aspecting 10th house says there will be a boy in the later stage of life (boy for karma) 4) Casual

Friendships occur now, it will result in marriage later on. 5) Overall your marriage life is not a big problem as feared by you in the question.

Date: **07/20/09**

57. POST GRADUATION IN MEDICINE, SURGERY.....:

Question:

My dob 05/05/1988 TOB 03.25 am POB Madurai Tamilnadu. Pisces lagna Scorpio Rasi Jeshtha Star 4th pada.I wish to record that I narrowly missed mbbs seat and studied BDS in 2005 and appeared for MBBS entrance of Pondicherry Government onc eagain and was successful in 2006 August .Presently I am studying final year MBBS in a private medical college in Pondicherry with financial support of Govt.of Pondicherry (1.5 lakhs per year to cover tution fees - applicable to all 250 govt.quota seats).My parents spend approximately less than Rs 50000 per year for my education . I am happy about it. I am expected to complete my internship in MBBS by December 2011. I am interested to pursue my postgraduate education in a reputed govt institutions such as AIIMS ,JIPMER AND State Government Colleges including Madras Medical college ,Stanley etc., . I have started to prepare for PG entrance examinations now. Please inform me could I be successful to get a PG seat during 2012-2014 in any one of the clinical subjects - medicine,surgery ,pediatrics ,anasthesianeurology ,radiology etc.,.I do not want PG education in non-clinical subjectS - anatomy , physiology ,pharmocology , forensic etc., .As all of you know ,PG entrance examinations are indeed highly competitive these days and without God's grace , any amount of hardwork may not suffice .Of course ,I have started to prepare systematically. I do not want to be a burden to my father(a Professor with DOB 06.08.1956 TOB 17.54 hours POB Virudhunagar) for my PG education. All I need is a merit seat during May 2012- May 2014 and a short stay in abroad for superspeciality and a government job subsequently after. I submit to all experts to read my birth chart and suggest me any remedies to achieve my goal .Also highlight me the health and financial prosperity of my father during the next 10 years .I am thankful to all of you for your divinely messages

From: -- Anonymous India
Date: **07/12/09**

Answer:

• Internet charting tells me your moon sign is Scorpio. Asc Pisces Star Jyeshta. You are running Venus Dasha and Jupiter Antara Dasha. When I was going through the chart and seeing the second, fifth(second best for any horoscope) and ninth house(the best for any horoscope) lords sitting in the best possible positions and Lagna and Karma house lord jupiter(although with kendrathipathya dosha which I think is diluted by a malific Sun's association)is in second position, I don't need to go any furhter. Yours is excellent chart. You talked about getting things after your efforts. The problem is Venus Dasa - Venus is the lord of 3rd and eighth houses for you.It is the most malefic. Mars in exalted position and Ketu in sixth aspected by Jupiter give you success in whatever you undertake.

Pisces **Asc**	Aries **Sun** **Jup**	Taurus **Mer**	Gemini **Ven**
Aquarius **Rahu**			Cancer
Capricorn **Mars**			Leo **Ketu**
Sagittarius **Sat**	Scorpio **Moon**	Libra	Virgo

- Transitory position, with Saturn shortly would go to your 11th house(Saturn's best 2 1/2 year period), Rahu in 3rd house, things are bright in that also. Internship, there is no problem.

- But when going further to end of April,2012 you will be running Sade Satti(7 1/2 nattu Sani)although your Dasa will be still Venus, I see some probs. But when you can choose your applications,etc. when saturn is in retrogade motion(when orbiting 12th house) and jupiter in good position and overall good transit, then chances are more. Ketu and Mars indicate Medicine or Surgery, respectively in PG.

- Yes 5th house lord in 9th indicates Bon Voyage

58. I SUSPECT THE WORK OF 2ND PHASE OF SADE SATI:

Question:

Last 2 years has been hard financially. Especially lot of unexpected expenses are there. I suspect it may be due to 2nd phase Sade sati. I live in US and would like to get your insights on how the next 3-4 years will be financially. Any advice/guidance would be appreciated

Date of Birth: 01-04-1958
Birth Time: 14:47 PM
Birth Place: Rajkot
Gender: male
From: -- Anonymous US (northern California)
Date: **07/12/09**

Answer:

- Cancer Asc. Moon sign Leo. Running Rahu Dasha and Saturn Antara dasha. Saturn is the lord of 7 and 8, it is in 6th house.4th house Rahu in conjunction with Jupiter.Jupiter also has two aspects 6th house is very bad but its lordship of 9th house is the best. You have Sade Satti as your Saturn is currently transiting the house number 1 from your natal Moon.

-

Pisces Sun	Aries Mer Ketu	Taurus	Gemini
Aquarius Ven			Cancer Asc
Capricorn Mars			Leo Moon
Sagittarius Sat	Scorpio	Libra Jup Rahu	Virgo

- Shortly when Saturn goes to house no.2 (although it is Sade Satti - it will relieve the problems/difficulties associated with these things for the next 2 years and 6 months: Friends, Wife,Job,lack of mental strength,long term finances etc. the direction to your future will be shown. I dont say your finance will be sorted, but the direction will be shown. There will be cash crunch, not medium term financial problem. After 2 1/2 years it is the best period for your finances, long term fulfilment of all you wanted.

- At that time your Dasa also will be helpful.

Date: **07/20/09**

59. BROKEN RELATIONSHIPS AND WORRIED:

Question:

- Date of Birth: 15-08-1985
Time of Birth:18:25
Place of Birth:New Delhi, India
Gender:female

- Date of Birth: 15-08-1985 Time of Birth: 18:25 Place of Birth:New Delhi Gender:female Hi, could some good astrology please predict/ tell me when will I get married and whats the best time? I've had some broken relationships and now I'm worried.

I'm a girl, my d.o.b. is 15th august 1985, time: 18:25, place: New Delhi, India. Also, will it be love/arranged? How will my married life be? Are there any particular planets that are afflicted, if so please offer remedies... I'll be highly obliged and thankful to everyone who takes this up! Thanks a tonne in advance! Any help would be highly appreciated!!

From: -- Anonymous India
Date: **07/12/09**

Answer:

Pisces	Aries **Rahu**	Taurus	Gemini **Ven**
Aquarius			Cancer **Sun** **Moon** **Mer** **Mars**
Capricorn **Asc** **Jup**			Leo
Sagittarius	Scorpio	Libra **Sat** **Ketu**	Virgo

- Capricon Asc. Jupiter in Asc. You have 4 planets in 7th house (house for marriage related matters) Sun,Moon, Mercury and Mars. Out of the four Moon is your 7th house lord as well. Therefore, there is no suprise in many relationships and breaks in them. Lagna Lord Saturn is in conjuction with Ketu in 10th house.And Suha sthana is occupied by Rahu. you are running Venus dasa and Venus Antara dasa. Venus is in 6th house. Still you are having Sade satti.

- After this year, things would brighten up. Generally dont worry too much about marriage life. Take it easy. Go about choosing your partner in a methodical manner through elders. As with so many planets in 7th house you tend to be emotional. You need an elder's support in choice of partner. Therefore arranged marriage is very much advised. Once married, to the right partner, matching horoscopes, there won't be problem in your married life.

-

Date: **07/20/09**

60. WHAT LINE FOR MY SON...:

Question:

This is for my son. He will be going to collect in 2012. Please advise 1) how his education will be in general 2) What line he should take (medicine, Business, engineering) Thanks

Date of Birth: 8-10-1994
Birth Time: 12:23 PM
Birth Place: San Jose
Gender: male

From: -- Anonymous US (northern California)
Date: **07/16/09**

Answer:

• Vedic Scholar charting Moon sign scorpio asc Scorpio Star Anuradha. Second and fifth lord Jupiter in twelfth house, with three planets –Venus (Mooltrikona), Mercury and Rahu. I have seen Jupiter alone in twelfth house would spoil the place. But here with Venus and Rahu he becomes competitive. Lagna karaka although in debilitation (se neechbhanga explanation) also sees them. Saturn in 4th in his own house (related to degree education) aspected by Jupiter. All indicate double major in degree. Moon in Scorpio and Mars in debilitation in cancer is for neechabhanga yoga to some extent. Ninth house lord Moon in Lagna gives lot of fame to the person.

Pisces	Aries **Ketu**	Taurus	Gemini
Aquarius **Sat**			Cancer **Mars**
Capricorn			Leo
Sagittarius	Scorpio **Asc** **Moon**	Libra **Mer** **Ven** **Jup** **Rahu**	Virgo **Sun**

- I would recommend Double major in degree with Business as first choice.

- Medicine comes next and Engineering third.

(NOTE for students: I earlier made a mistake in charting —another

astrologer pointed out that mistake- Pl.note USA regions are divided into Easter, Central, Western Pacific, Alaska, USA Hawaii – Adjustments in zone need be made – but it is taken care of a really good software- Another point is about Day light saving regions – Please look for Summer adjustments in many countries- another point is about War time adjustments)

Date: **07/20/09**

61. MAYA OF HURDLES AT THE LAST MOMENT FOR JOBS:

Question:

Currenlty in pune. I am looking for a job change.I am getting new jobs but some hurdles are coming to prevent me getting it finally (even after clearing interview).When will I be successful? What kind of job will be suitable for me? Whether I can do higher studies (MBA).If yes when? Pleasae tell me about my marriage date & partner? I am getting hurdles & problems in all aspects of my life...

- Date of Birth: 10-08-1984
  Birth Time: 08-45 A M

Birth Place: Tiruchirappalli
Gender: male

From: -- A.P. pune
Date: **07/12/09**

Answer

Moon Sign Capricorn Ascendant sign is Virgo.Your Birth Star is Uttara Shadya. You are currently running Rahu Dasha and Saturn Antardasha.

Pisces	Aries	Taurus **Rahu**	Gemini
Aquarius			Cancer **Sun**
Capricorn **Moon**			Leo **Mer** **Ven**
Sagittarius **Jup**	Scorpio **Mars** **Ketu**	Libra **Sat**	Virgo **Asc**

- Rahu in 9th house hurts good chances and Saturn in 2nd house leads you in lower positions than you want. Rahu dasha is supposed to take the native to foreign countries.But being in 9th house (9th house is the house for foreign travel) he delays your journey for some time. In transitory positions, you have scored 5 out of maximum possible 9. On the whole this time is 55.56% good for you. Jupiter is in good position. Ashtama Sani is creating problems.Rahu, mercury andhara dasha will be better.

- You will get a job but it may not be to your liking. In the recession time take up anything that comes up. You will take MBA in 2011 June. To ward of Ashtama Sani go to or Pray to Thirunallar Saneeswar.

Date: 07/19/09

62. MY MARS, HER MARS AND OUR MARS:

Question:

Date of Birth: 28-02-1977
Time of Birth: 05:05 am
Place of Birth: Hyderabad
Gender: male

My name: C... Girls name: Che.. My DOB & TIME: 28/02/77 & 05:05am Girls DOB & time: 24/09/83 &

07:15am both of our birth places: Hyderabad. Can you please help to clarify the below: (1) My mars is in lagnam and her mars is in 12th house is it safe to get married as i believe both of us are magliks (kuja dosham) but some astrologer told that effect of mars in my horoscope is only 25%, but it is 100% in girls horoscope. Are these kujadoshams still they are getting nullified? And okey for marriage? (2) Are they any pariharams/ homams/ shanthis that the girl or I have to perform? If so, on what days of the week or when exactly these should be performed? (3)Will our married life be gud? And will it affect our social life or economic status and could you also confirm if it would affect our potential children? (4) I have been trying for proposals for quite some time but marriage is getting settled but at the last moment they are getting canceled with no mistake from mine. I am just worried if this would turn out to be like one of these cases, please advise if okay to proceed with this proposal. (5) Could you please fix two nearest murthams for Engagement and marriage in year 2009 & confirm if the girls name has to be changed, if so, what should her name start with? From: -- Anonymous Hyderabad Date: 07/19/09**Answer:**

Pisces **Ven**	Aries **Ketu**	Taurus **Jup**	Gemini **Moon**
Aquarius **Sun** **Mer**			Cancer **Sat**
Capricorn **Asc** **Mars**			Leo
Sagittarius	Scorpio	Libra **Rahu**	Virgo

Pisces **Moon**	Aries	Taurus **Rahu**	Gemini
Aquarius			Cancer
Capricorn			Leo **Mer** **Ven** **Mars**
Sagittarius	Scorpio **Jup** **Ketu**	Libra **Sat**	Virgo **Asc** **Sun**

Some preliminary recap Your Porutham score is 25.5/36 which is excellent.100% on Gana, Bakoota and Naadi Poruththams. The ego aspect covered by Varna is missing. Vashya (mutual attraction) is 25% Health and Bilogical compatability (Taara and Yoni)are 50%. I am concerned only about the intellectual level. You both need to give importance to other's views on worldly affairs. 1. What you heard is that your Kuja Dosh is only 25% because of two things: one aspect of Jupiter and another aspect of Saturn. But some consider that when Mars is in exhalted position in Capricorn there is no dosha at all. I subscribe to the later view.For the girl it is 12th house- Leo- with Venus and Mercury along with MARS.Here opinions differ. Kuja associated with benefic planets is considered to have less dosha or no dosha. If we take the notion of Kuja not losing its dosha with benefic planets then Kuja Dosha from 12th house is about financial losses, enemies.Your strong Mars (ascendent) nullifies those things. Therefore, Kuja dosha shouldn't be analysed in isolation. After analysing your horoscopes in detail as mentioned above I strongly say any dosha is nullified and you can proceed with the marriage.

No.	Koota	Meaning	Max. Score	Your Score
1	Varna	Indicates ego development between the partners.	1	0
2	Vashya	Indicates the intensity of mutual attraction and affection between the couple.	2	0.5
3	Taara	Indicates the health, longevity and well-being of the couple.	3	1.5
4	Yoni	Indicates biological compatibility and satisfaction.	4	2
5	Graha-Maitri	Indicates compatibility in outlook, objective, intellectual level and spiritual plane of existence.	5	0.5
6	Gana	Indicates the compatibility of temperamental characteristics.	6	6
7	Bhakoota	Indicates Socio Economic Status, Progenic happiness, growth of the family and family-welfare	7	7
8	Naadi	Signifies the duration of married life, the health(outward physique) and constitution(internal metabolism).	8	8
Total			36	25.5

- 2.As per the above I dont see any pariharms required, but to bring propserity to your family you can do a Navagraha Homam with emphasis on Budha, her asc lord who is in 12th house.

- 3)100% sure, you will have a happy long married life.

- 4) It is not the Mars. It was the Saturn sitting in 7th house that delayed your marriage. In Transition Now Jupiter in 9 and Saturn in 3. You are running Jupiter Dasha and Rahu Antardasha. Jupiter in 5th house and Rahu in 10th house are very good. This is the period for your marriage,stick with proposal/s. 5) a) KARTHIGAI 20 06-12-2009 sunday panchami poosam siddha yogam 06.00 to 07.00 am vrichika lagnam b) AVANI 21 06..09.2009 SUNDAY DWETHIYAI UTHRATTAHI AMIRTHA YOGAM 09.00 TO 10.30 AM THULA LAGNAM . No Name change required

•

Date: **07/19/09**

63. ADOPTION OF TWO YOUNG GIRLS:

Question:

We have currently launched a procedure to adopt two young girls from India, and I would love to know what the astrology expert's advice would be. Many thanks in advance. Best regards D......

Date of Birth: 29/01/1967
Birth Time: 04:52 a.m.
Birth Place: Aalen Germany
Gender: female
From: -- D.... Paris, France
Date: **07/13/09**

Answer:

• Although I liked to have both horoscopes, I go according to what is given.

• Your place is Aalen, GER: 48n50, 10e05, 29/01/1967 4.52 am. I cast the horoscope on http://vedicscholar.com...

• In Indian Vedic Astrology Your Moon sign is Leo.The zodiac sign in which the moon was located at the time of your birth is known as Moon sign. Vedic astrology places special emphasis on the Moon sign.

Your Ascendant sign is Scorpio. Your star is Purva Phalguni.

Pisces **Sat**	Aries **Rahu**	Taurus	Gemini
Aquarius **Ven**	29/01/1967 04:52 a.m. Aalen Germany		Cancer **Jup**
Capricorn **Sun** **Mer**			Leo **Moon**
Sagittarius	Scorpio **Asc**	Libra **Mars** **Ketu**	Virgo

- There are several aspects that decide about children as well as adopted children. For ladies it is fifth and ninth house from asc. Saturn is considered a malific planet which will affect the house in which it is placed, but at the end will give the benefits of the house in an indirect way. That's why you had problems about own children. Saturn is considered helpful for people who are helping the needy and destitues. Therefore the Saturn's 5th house occupany indicates a definite case for adoption. Coming to the 9th house which indicates the happiness associated with children, which is occupied by Jupiter which Astrology considers the most benefic planet. Therefore any adoption will bring much needed satisfaction and happiness in your life. Apart from that Jupiter can aspect(see) the ninth house from where it is. This aspect falls on the fifth house and on Saturn. I see the previous statements doubly strengthened.

- Apart from positions of planets, in Indian Astrology there is another element called Dasha (Periods of Planetary rules). The planets are supposed to give their results either in their Dasa or Antaradasha. You are running Rahu Dasa(period) and Moon Antaradasha(sub period). In your chart Rahu is powerful and sixth position from Asc is very good and success in whatever you undertake. Aries itself is good place for Rahu. Moon is the lord of the 9th house (Cancer) and sits in 10(tenth), Ninth house is considered the most auspicious in a chart. Ninth house lord sitting in 10th house(10th house is in one way indicates children who will take care of the native in their later years)again asserts my earlier view.

- People with Leo moon sign, will go through proper processes, do everything according to book and as instructed by authorities.That's what you are doing and will be successful. Now I introduce one more element in Indian astrology that of Transition of planets,as per your current planetary position Rahu is in 6th house too, that is one of the best for Rahu in 18 years and Jupiter is in 7th house is auspiscious, although Saturn in 1st house affects self confidence and separation, I see that anything done for the good of others will not be affected by Saturn's position. The procedure will take some time because of Saturn. I advise to keep the documentation and procedures as far as possible, crystal clear. You need to concentrate on financial aspects and make provisions to satisfy the authorities.At the end it is long time mental satisfaction.

-

Date: **07/19/09**

64. 13 YEAR LOVE, MY PARENTS GAVE GREEN SIGNAL WHAT ABOUT HERS:

Question:

Date of Birth: 05-05-1981
Time of Birth: 03-50 AM
Place of Birth:Coimbatore
Gender:male

- Hi Ammas, I am in a difficult situation right now.My DOB is 05-05-1981 at 3.50 AM in Coimbatore; Tamilnadu.I love one girl sincerely from the past 13 years. Right now I am running Rahu dasa Sani Bhukti.My parents gave the green signal for my love. Could you plz tell me whether my love was successful and my marriage will happen with her. Rajesh...

From: -- r..... Tamilnad

Answer:

I look first at Transitory Positions now. I got a prasna lagna of Taurus as well as your Rasi is Taurus. Major Planets: Jupiter in 10, Saturn in 4, Rahu Mars 9, and 1 respectively are not good generally. When mars and Saturn are in retrogade motion, they produce results as if they are in 3 and 12. Sun in 3

Venus in 1 are good. Mercury in 3 and Moon in 2 are not good. You have scored 7 out of maximum possible 9. On the whole this week or so is 77.78% good for you. As per Prasna I will say this is real good thing to happen at this time.

- Secondly looking at your chart with Pisces Ascendant and Taurus Rasi Kriththikja star (South indian Tradition vedicscholar casting)Yoga karaka Rahu in Poorva Punniya sthana -5th (cancer) and Saturn(your Laab Sthanathipathi 11th house and Nithra house lord(12th house) in spouse's place 7th (Virgo)in conjucnction with sahala papa Nivarana(your Lagna and 10th house lord) Jupiter, tells me you will be successful in your marriage.I had concerns that Jupiter has Kendrathipathya dosha, that is, benefic planets having 1,4,7,10 lordship. As Jupiter in 7th is in retro, this is solved.

Pisces **Asc**	Aries **Sun** **Mer** **Ven** **Mars**	Taurus **Moon**	Gemini
Aquarius	05-05-1981 03-50 AM Coimbatore **11n0, 76e58**		Cancer **Rahu**
Capricorn **Ketu**			Leo
Sagittarius	Scorpio	Libra	Virgo **Jup** **Sat**

- Rahu in 1, 4, 5,7,10 and 11th house and aspected by a benefic will give promotion and increased income). There may be occasional hurdles and problems in progress. Fear and anger of those in high places, problems due to immovable assets and anxiety related to house and land are possible.

- In Saturn Antara Dasa If Saturn is in 1st, 4th, 7th or 10th house then it gives the native good results (7th house - marriage) after a lot of hurdles.

I go one more step and analyse the Stars in which Rahu and Saturn sit.

Rahu is the most difficult planet for even the most learned Astrologers. But Krishnamurthi Paththathi, T.R.Balu, or B.V. Raman all have some thing in common about Rahu. I come to that within. Rahu is in Poosam, Saturn's star. Rahu will give the effects of the planet of the star in which it is in. As Saturn is in 7th house it will give Saturn's results, that of Profit (11th house) and night pleasure (12th house) and Marriage. Saturn in Hastha gives the full effects of 5th house (Moon)-Poorva Punya.Moon is Mind Karaka. That's why you get all kind of fears and anxiety. I can say they are all imaginary and you will succeed in your marriage.
Date: **07/19/09**

RANKING OF R.S. AS ON 13-1-2010 IN CATEGORIES IN AMMAS

Category	Rank
Featured Council	
Astrology	21
Australia	1
Baby Names	1
Business	54
Career	2
Career Advice	3
Cricket	1
Current Affairs	3
Design and Programming	1
Diseases	1
Divorce	2
Film and TV Production	1
Financial Markets	1
Foreign Exchange	1
Gateway To The U.S.	1
General Cultures and Groups	1
Global Economy	1
Government	1
Health	2
Health Insurance	1

History	3
Hobbies	1
Holidays	1
Immigration	1
Income Tax	1
India	1
Information Technology	3
Investing	2
Issues and Causes	19
Marriage	2
New Zealand	1
Other_Lifestyle and Living	1
People	3
Personals	3
Philosophy	1
Poetry	1
Polls and Surveys	2
Travel	15
Travel Insurance	1
TV Shows	7
USA	19
Work From Home	1